Win Keep Grow

Endorsements

Mark masterfully removes the complexity from subscription pricing strategies and distills it into frameworks anyone can understand and apply to their business. If you are growing your subscription business or looking to shift your revenues from cost-plus pricing to value-based pricing strategies, this book will be your handy guide. I am a subject matter expert in subscription pricing and Mark has given me a structured way to think about and communicate my pricing strategies to the colleagues and stakeholders I work with. I continually find myself going back to his frameworks throughout my career.

Natalie Louie, Pricing Strategist and Senior
Director of Product Marketing at Zuora

The world is changing at an incredible pace. To avoid disruption and survive, business leaders need to innovate quickly and create monetization models that support their innovation strategy. That's where *Win Keep Grow* comes into play. Mark Stiving has developed a robust and comprehensive guide to subscription models. He goes beyond the hype and dives deep into the benefits and the mechanics of implementing a subscription. Whether your company focuses on software, hardware, or both (such as IoT), this book is a mandatory read for any leader driving innovation.

Daniel Elizalde, Former VP, Head of IoT at
Ericsson & Instructor at Stanford University

Comprehensive, yet concise, Mark Stiving's *Win Keep Grow* distills what every business needs to know to make the transition to subscription based pricing. In his clear style, Mark challenges the reader to think along with him throughout the book. I found myself running through the exercises and having lightbulbs flash like the sky during a fireworks show. This book won't just sit on a shelf, but be your companion on your desk.

Ed Kless, Co-host of *The Soul of Enterprise*

This book is a must-read for anyone considering a subscription model for their software product. It exposes the reader to the fundamentals like pricing. It also contains the not-so-fundamentals like transitioning your organization or your customers to a subscription-based business. The book is chock full of practical advice and suggestions. Read it to increase your chances of success. Ignore it — you're doomed. Don't ignore it.

Jim Geisman, Founder of Software Pricing Partners and Growth-Helper

Win, Keep, Grow is a brilliant and thoughtful guide for anyone pursuing success in the world of subscriptions. Mark invites and challenges the reader to consider more than just the subscription business model itself, but also the critical roles of pricing and value. As an educator at heart, his approach has produced a book that is as supportive as it is informative, and as practical as it is theoretical — calling on decades of experience and insight.

Courtney Rogers, CEO of Court & Co.

For over 10 years, Mark Stiving and his work in pricing has been an influential asset to my executive career. If you get it right, pricing is an incredibly powerful tool. When you get it wrong, you find out quickly how this power is balanced by incredible product, business, fiscal and career risk. For myself, my teams, advisory clients and for dozens of my colleagues, Mark, his courses, his first book, and his Podcast have helped me control risks and win in pricing, whether it was for one product or for my entire portfolio. *Win, Keep, Grow: How to Price, Package and Manage Subscriptions* is packed with wisdom, stellar examples and clear guidance that will help everyone, at all skill levels, with making the most out of the subscription business model. A few hours with this book will not only save you time and make you and your customers more successful, but you will also find it to be a quick and enjoyable read — a rarity in business books these days.

Michael Fox, VP Product, Author,
SaaS & Mobile Entrepreneur

I can't think of a more misunderstood and poorly executed pricing tactic between a customer and a vendor than subscription-based pricing. As always, Mark's book is at the forefront of addressing a need so timely in today's turbulent and chaotic economic environment. Mark's message is clear and concise by reminding readers that subscription pricing is about capturing experiential value as perceived by customers followed by the need to understand their willingness-to-pay. In a way, Mark's insights remind us that Subscription pricing is an ongoing covenant between two parties extending beyond the initial sale. To succeed, a vendor must continue to innovate and communicate value and, in return the customer reciprocates with payments often extending over a 2 or 3 year commitment. Mark's book is a must read for anyone considering a viable alternative to traditional pricing approaches.

Michael N. Hurwich, President Strategic
Pricing Management Group

The book title explains it all: *WIN, KEEP, and GROW*. Each represents a different stage in the product life cycle; each must be priced, packaged and measured differently. In particular, focus your attention on the three value levers: market segments, pricing metrics, and packaging. These are often chosen tacitly without understanding their impact on the business, which is why the chapter on Value Levers is a must-read. Subscription isn't just a pricing decision; it's a strategic business model decision. That's why product leaders need to read *Win Keep Grow*, the latest book from pricing expert Mark Stiving.

Steve Johnson, Chief Product Officer
Under10 Consulting

Mark Stiving is a pricing expert, but *Win Keep Grow: How to Price and Package to Accelerate Your Subscription Business* showcases his expertise in the subscription business model. Subscription business isn't a payment plan, it's a business model; different expertises become critical to success.

The one that strikes closest to home for me is that subscription businesses need to become crystal clear on their customer's business, and the outcomes that their product helps customers achieve. Outcomes are the foundation of your value. Knowing your customer outcomes drives sales, marketing, pricing, product, packaging, and your product development/enhancement strategies, and Mark's book describes how. Great Read!

Mark Boundy, Author of *Radical Value*

If you're thinking about adding a subscription channel to your business, this book is a "Must Read". Mark Stiving shares the behind-the-scenes insights that differentiate successful subscription companies from those that disappear overnight. The key is how Mark expertly establishes the critical link between price and value that so many miss. With the exercises included at the end of each chapter, readers can identify real-life best practices and then apply them to their own business. I learned a lot and I'm sure others will too.

Brian Doyle, President, Holden Advisors

Disruptive threats come not from new technology but from new business models. Fairly soon, you will have the option to subscribe to nearly everything, from boats and cars, to guitars and clothes. Your business will have to deal with this reality, regardless of whether or not it offers a subscription relationship. In *Win Keep Grow*, pricing expert Mark Stiving offers exceptional counsel on how to navigate in these new waters. We simply have to change our mindset from selling guitars to helping our customers play the guitar better; teasing out what it is our customers truly value, and constantly innovating to enhance our customer's success.

Ronald J. Baker, Radio-Show Host, *The Soul of Enterprise: Business in the Knowledge Economy*, and author of the best-selling book, *Implementing Value Pricing: A Radical Business Model for Professional Firms* www.thesoulofenterprise.com

Mark's skill as an instructor comes through in this well-written, actionable book. I'd recommend it for any subscription practitioner wanting to build a forever transaction with their customers. It's easy to understand and full of specific exercises to bring complex concepts to life."

Robbie Kellman Baxter, Author of *The Forever Trasanction* & *The Membership Economy*

How we buy and how we sell has changed. We're living in an "Everything-as-a-Service" world where things that were once out of reach for most because of price are now all of a sudden affordable as a subscription. While subscriptions have made it easier for buyers to buy, they have demanded new monetization techniques from the companies that offer them. Mark Stiving is the perfect guide to this new world where subscription pricing and packaging can help keep your customers in and your competitors out.

Ryan Glushkoff, Founder of Fraction8

WIN
KEEP
GROW

How to Price and Package
to ACCELERATE Your
Subscription Business

Mark Stiving Ph.D.

NEW YORK

LONDON • NASHVILLE • MELBOURNE • VANCOUVER

WIN KEEP **GROW**

How to Price and Package to Accelerate Your Subscription Business

Published in New York, New York, by Morgan James Publishing. Morgan James is a trademark of Morgan James, LLC. www.MorganJamesPublishing.com

Morgan James BOGO™

A **FREE** ebook edition is available for you or a friend with the purchase of this print book.

CLEARLY SIGN YOUR NAME ABOVE

Instructions to claim your free ebook edition:
1. Visit MorganJamesBOGO.com
2. Sign your name CLEARLY in the space above
3. Complete the form and submit a photo of this entire page
4. You or your friend can download the ebook to your preferred device

ISBN 9781631954788 paperback
ISBN 9781631954795 eBook
Library of Congress Control Number: 2020952647

Cover and Interior Design by:
Chris Treccani
www.3dogcreative.net

Morgan James PUBLISHING Builds with... **Habitat for Humanity®** Peninsula and Greater Williamsburg

Morgan James is a proud partner of Habitat for Humanity Peninsula and Greater Williamsburg. Partners in building since 2006.

Get involved today! Visit
MorganJamesPublishing.com/giving-back

To Carol and Jake

Table of Contents

Acknowledgments

It is impossible for me to create a book on my own. I owe a debt of gratitude to many people, some of whom I mention here.

Theresa French: Thank you for thinking through the strategy with me and for keeping me motivated throughout the process. Your focus on the business enables me to create content.

Courtney Rogers and Jim Schibler: Thank you for your editing. Your honest feedback and keen eyes made this a much better book.

Natalie Louie Kao: Thank you for sharing your immense expertise on subscriptions while I was formulating these frameworks and for poking holes in them as they were created. Your knowledge and experience are invaluable.

Ron Baker and Ed Kless: Thank you for getting me excited about subscriptions in your show The Soul of Enterprise. Hearing your thoughts and enthusiasm helped me realize what an important, interesting, and misunderstood topic subscription business is.

Morgan James Publishing: Thank you for your enthusiastic support of this project. Your guidance has been incredible.

Jake: Thank you for cajoling me to leave my office and get exercise every day. You made me take time to just think. (woof, woof)

Carol Stiving: Thank you for loving me and taking so many burdens from me. You gave me the motivation and opportunity to focus.

Preface

I have been studying, practicing and teaching pricing most of my life. It is an incredible topic because it has such an impact on a company's profitability, yet so few people understand it. My approach to pricing is based on how buyers make decisions using their perceptions of value and price.

While writing my doctoral thesis at UC Berkeley, "An Economic Theory of Pricing Endings," I became fascinated with how people use and perceive prices. I went on to create a semester long course to teach MBA's while a professor at The Ohio State University.

The role of value and how everyone contributes to it became crystal clear when I co-founded, grew, and sold a company in the early 2000's.

My next role, a pricing "executive" in a big company, taught me many things. The most important lessons were how everyone in the company is concerned about pricing, but nobody controlled all of it. Everyone influences how much value a buyer perceives, but almost nobody realizes it. Most importantly, nobody really understands the value of their products.

I created a pricing course that I taught to entrepreneurs and corporations, and eventually sold a version of it to Pragmatic Institute, where I became an instructor. It was there that I internalized the roles of product management and product marketing and how crucial they are to creating and communicating value. It was like finding the keys that unlock the secrets of value.

In 2019, I created Impact Pricing, an LLC dedicated to helping companies solve pricing problems through education and guidance. It gives me the freedom to do what that I love: helping others while sharing what I've learned.

I wrote this book because while studying subscriptions, I was bombarded with aha moments. My experience is in traditional businesses and was fascinated by how subscriptions differ in pricing, packaging and many strategic decisions. This book is my attempt to share many of these new thoughts.

Introduction

The subscription business model is taking the world by storm. Subscription-based companies grow much faster than their traditional counterparts, the business tends to be less cyclical, the lifetime value of a customer is higher, and buyers seem to love them too. Salesforce kicked off this trend in a big way, being the first major CRM company that was "born in the cloud." After Salesforce led the way, Adobe® was an early major company to shift from selling perpetual licenses to selling subscriptions. Microsoft® is another large company to transform most of its products, including the pervasive Office Suite, into subscriptions. Most companies I talk with have either shifted toward a subscription model or are trying to figure out how to do it.

From about 2014 to 2018, students in my pricing classes would ask, "how is pricing for subscriptions different to other business models?" I'd always answer, "It's the same. You still have to look at how the buyer values your product." I was right, but I was also naive.

Yes, you still have to look at how the buyer values your product. Price and value are critical in the buyer's decision process. But in traditional businesses, most buyers only buy once. They may buy again later or buy some accessory products, but the main event is a single purchase; this accounts for most of the sales revenue generated. Because of this, traditional businesses focus mostly on winning the next sale from the next customer.

In contrast, buyers decide to buy a subscription initially and then repeatedly buy (pay). They often don't make a new buying decision; they just pay to keep it going. Some buyers increase how much they buy over time. These simple nuances may not make the underlying concepts of pricing different, but they are so impactful to business results, it's hard to call them nuances. They rightfully influence the decisions companies must make around pricing and value, so subscription companies must understand them.

This book is about way more than you might think it is. You may think it's about putting a price on a product when you use a subscription business. After all, I'm a pricing expert. However, this book is about using what we know about pricing and value to make better, more profitable decisions in your subscription business.

By the way, whenever I use the word "product" in this book, I'm referring to whatever you sell. It could be a physical product, a service, software — anything a buyer pays money for. Using the word product simplifies my writing and your reading.

Also, I use the phrases "traditional business" and "traditional product" frequently. These refer to businesses and products that are NOT subscription-based. In the hardware world, buyers of traditional products purchase by the unit — for example, cars, printers, and hamburgers. In software, traditional products are commonly called perpetual licenses. That is, the buyer bought the right to use the product forever. Traditional is not bad; it is merely a word I use to mean non-subscription.

This book guides you on how to manage the value you deliver using a subscription business model. You will have many aha moments. (At least I had a lot of them as I delved deeply into the topic.) And you will learn a structure for how to think about and manage your business. Essentially, this book focuses on what and why. If you want more in-depth knowledge around the how-to, I created online courses on how to make many of the decisions described in this book. You can see these courses at www.impactpricing.com.

Section 1.

Fundamentals of Managing Subscriptions

You might not think subscriptions are your grandfather's business model — but just wait — maybe they are. Subscriptions have been around for a long time. The earliest subscription I am aware of was in the 1500s when European map makers sold subscriptions to map updates (*The Automatic Customer: Creating a Subscription Business in Any Industry* by John Warrillow). However, the rapid adoption of the subscription pricing and business model indicates something powerful may be happening right now. And it is.

These first four chapters build a framework for understanding subscriptions. They describe why subscriptions are so powerful and the essential tools you need to manage them. Even if you have experience with subscriptions, please don't skip these chapters. You will learn an easy way to think about subscriptions, and you'll be more able to discuss subscriptions with others using this framework.

1

The Motivation

———————◆———————

A subscription is *a periodic payment in exchange for recurring benefits of a product*. Periodic could mean weekly, monthly, quarterly, or annually. Regardless of which period you choose, one of the keys to successful subscription businesses is automating the customer's payment so they don't even think about whether or not they should continue paying. It's similar to having a direct deposit of your paycheck.

The phrase "recurring benefits" explains why the most outstanding subscription businesses thrive. When they sell their product, the customer doesn't receive ownership; instead, they receive *temporary access* to the product. The company needs to make sure the customer continues to receive significant benefits so they will continue as a subscriber.

Subscriptions may seem like a new phenomenon, but they aren't new. We've had subscriptions around us our entire lives. Before the Internet, we subscribed to gyms, newspapers, cable TV, and phone service (landlines, of course). Even Business to Business (B2B) subscriptions pre-dated the Internet: with companies like Dun and Bradstreet, who provided information to salespeople about potential customers; and Xerox Corporation, who sold subscriptions to service their copy machines.

Salesforce may not be the first software as a Service (SaaS) company utilizing the Internet to replace traditional ("shrink-wrapped," "on-premises") offerings, but they are indeed the poster child. Their runaway success caught the attention of other companies, which prompted a movement. Today, almost all software companies — and even many hardware companies — are trying to figure out how to shift to a subscription business model.

As it turns out, you can turn almost any business into a subscription and make it a service business. At the Dollar Shave Club, you can pay a monthly fee and have your razors and accessories shipped directly to your house. Of course, this is because of the consumable nature of the products. But what about cars? Believe it or not, you can subscribe to Porsche. In Atlanta, for $3,000 per month, you could drive any Porsche any day. You can drive a Cayenne on the weekend to go skiing and a 911 on weekdays to drive to work. Did you know you can even subscribe to a doctor? This is not insurance; it's premium access to your doctor for routine or specialized health services.

Even if your company is not strictly a subscription business, there may be much to learn from this book. Products like Uber, Lyft, AWS, and Azure do not fit the subscription model because users pay per use. Yet, every one of these products' success requires onboarding customers, frequent repeat business, and growing usage — three critical characteristics of subscriptions. While studying subscriptions, I have learned many lessons applicable to both subscription-based and traditional companies. For example, a SaaS business must choose a pricing metric (what to charge for). Also, traditional companies may be able to create disruptive new business models by rethinking their pricing metrics. Of course, there are many more lessons to learn and uncover, both in this book and beyond.

Why Subscriptions?

You may be wondering what causes the incredible growth seen in subscription businesses. The simple answer is subscriptions are valuable to both the buyer and the seller (company). Let's dig into both.

Why Buyers Love Subscriptions

We all subscribe to something today. We subscribe to cell phones, TV or video services, music services, news outlets, gym memberships... and that's before we get to software services like Microsoft Office, a sales CRM, and any of the (literally) thousands of marketing tools to which you could subscribe. At last count, Impact Pricing subscribes to over 20 services to help run our website, marketing, and product delivery.

We may be getting subscription overload, but we still love subscriptions. Here's why.

Buyers buy the benefit, not the product. In the old days, we would buy a product and receive something tangible. Do you remember when software was a set of physical disks and a manual shrink wrapped in a box? We were purchasing an object; we hoped the item solved a problem for us, but we bought the object. Beyond the purchase price, the object sometimes came with many additional costs, including shipping, storage, installation, insurance, maintenance, and disposal.

In the world of subscriptions, we don't buy objects. We buy the benefits we gain by using a product. We are much clearer on what we need: the hole, not the drill.

I recently signed up for LastPass, a password management service. While shopping, I wasn't thinking, "I need to buy a program to manage passwords." No. I was thinking, "I need to find a way to make it easy for dad and me to share and manage passwords." I was shopping for the benefit.

Think about the Porsche subscription. Do people really want to own a Porsche, with all of the maintenance, upkeep, and rapid depreciation? Or, do they want to drive a Porsche whenever they want? Most people probably care more about driving it, or being seen in it, than actually owning it.

Subscriptions are logical and straightforward. From a user's perspective, we can get up and running on a new product and start receiving the desired benefit relatively quickly. It is rare to subscribe to something with a long learning curve.

It turns out this is by design. When a company wins a new customer, they want the customer to stay — but customers only continue subscribing if they get value out of your product, and fast. Hence, companies make their products easy for beginners to get value quickly so they don't want to leave. Customers who don't use the product will stop subscribing. In the jargon of subscriptions: companies have onboarding programs to minimize the customer's time to value, which helps reduce churn (cancellation of subscriptions).

Buyers get faster time to value, meaning the product is doing something useful quickly (such as solving the customer's problem). This is way better than slogging through a manual to figure out how to use a complex software package.

Subscriptions provide flexibility to grow. Users often start with a small amount of a subscribed service, but they know they can get more as they use it and love it. Buyers want to learn more about the benefits available to them as they need it. This is especially true for business buyers. As a company grows, they want the product to continue to support them.

Subscription-based companies build this into their products in many ways. Buyers can pay based on some usage metric (so as they use more, they pay more). Buyers can upgrade to a more feature-rich version of the product. Or, buyers can buy different yet compatible products to expand the capabilities of their current subscription. These become more relevant to subscription companies as they scale.

Subscriptions reduce risk. We can subscribe to something for a nominal entry price to see if it provides the benefits we expected — and as buyers, we LOVE this. In the old days, we had to commit the total amount of money upfront before using the product. We just *hoped* the product purchase performed as we expected. Now, we buy for a month or two, and if it doesn't meet or exceed our needs, we stop paying and are only out a much smaller amount.

Subscription products are better. To ensure customers renew their subscriptions, sellers need to deliver value quickly and continually. They can't get away with poor performance; their customers are not 'stuck' with the product. If the customer decides they don't like it, they can cut off the recurring payment at any time. Thus, providers of subscription products MUST maintain high levels of customer satisfaction. This imperative tends to drive higher product usability, performance, and reliability than the norms seen with traditional products.

Because of this, when we subscribe to a new offer, the product is probably better than if we had bought a solution outright. Yet, over the life of the product, it will get even better. Vendors add more features and capabilities to ensure we're receiving more value over time, so we maintain our subscription. We often get vastly more than what we originally bought.

B2B customers can more easily calculate ROI. We subscribe to solve a problem that has some cost to us. If we can measure the cost of the problem, we can measure the value of the benefit and compare it to the price of the solution. This is much easier to do when paying periodically than when buying a product outright and attempting to amortize the price over a long-yet-mystical timeframe.

B2B accounting is more accessible and more beneficial. Subscription payments come out of operating expenses, the other benefit applicable to business buyers. Expensive purchases (i.e., not subscriptions) are considered capital expenses. Capital expenses are harder to account for; they require depreciation tables and the application of complex accounting rules. Conversely, operating expenses are generally tax-deductible immediately, whereas capital expenses are not.

From a customer's perspective, the only real **disadvantage** to a subscription is we often pay *more* over time. This is especially painful with older products that no longer need significant improvements. Say we subscribe to Microsoft Word. Ten or even twenty years ago, Word probably had every feature we use today. We don't need it to be any better — still we pay the subscription. We would probably be just as productive on Office 97 (if it would run). Paying $10 per month for ten years is $1,200, which seems pretty expensive. However, in this rapidly changing world — for most products — a subscription is a much better decision for customers. For example, if you subscribe to Netflix, much of the value comes from the new content you expect them to create or acquire in the future.

Why Sellers Love Subscriptions

More and more companies are offering subscriptions. Major companies like Microsoft and Adobe have already transitioned to subscriptions, and others, including Hewlett-Packard Enterprise and Dell Computer, have committed to transitioning to subscriptions as well. Subscriptions are becoming an increasingly popular business model for three significant reasons: faster growth, higher lifetime value of a customer, and higher valuations of their market capitalization. Let's look at each of these reasons in more detail.

Faster Growth

Research shows subscription-based companies are growing much more rapidly than the Fortune 500. Perhaps you could argue it's because the Fortune 500 companies are larger and less agile, but there are some significant reasons why subscription companies grow faster.

First, buyers have **lower entry costs**, so it's easier to win new customers. Buyers don't have to commit to a considerable upfront expense. Companies can often win new customers without salespeople or the buyer's purchasing people getting involved; this is a business model commonly referred to as *product-led growth*.

Second, as long as companies keep new customers happy, **they continue to pay**. Subscription companies essentially start the year out with whatever sales they ended with last year (minus churn). Therefore, each new sale is incremental revenue. Contrast this to a traditional business, where each year starts at zero, and they have to hustle most of the year just to match the previous year's revenue. It's common for a subscription company to book 70% of its annual revenue on January 1!

Third, subscription-based companies earn more revenue as their **customers grow and use more of their products**. In traditional businesses, once the deal is closed, salespeople immediately start chasing the next sale. The customer has paid them, so they don't care how much — or even if — the customer uses their product. However, subscription companies *need* to help their customers be more successful by using the product continually — because the more the customer uses it, the more revenue the company makes.

Higher Lifetime Value

Subscription-based companies have a higher average Lifetime Value (LTV) per customer. There is a formula for LTV in chapter 4. For now, think of LTV as the total profit a company makes from a single customer across all purchase events. In subscriptions, once a customer buys in, the seller works hard to keep that customer happy and paying, using techniques like fixing bugs and adding new capabilities. They monitor evolving customer needs and solve new problems. **They build better relationships because they care**. They *really* care. Unlike a traditional business, in which they care until they get the order (or maybe a little longer), they must care forever in a subscription business!

Subscription businesses also have higher LTV because **customers tend to be more sticky**. As long as the subscription product is continually improved and continues to solve the user's problems, the customer doesn't need or want to shop for a new solution. Switching costs (such as installation, learning, training) are often high, and as long as the subscription product is working well, there's no reason in the customer's mind to incur those switching costs. Finally, making these decisions is hard. Nobody likes doing it. As long as the subscription continues to solve the customer's problem, inertia keeps the customer subscribed.

Another reason LTV is higher is that successful **subscription companies focus on growing revenue from their existing customers**. Yes, they have to win and keep a customer, but they can also *grow* the revenue they receive from them. As they build a great relationship and provide quality solutions and support, the customer trusts them and relies on them. As this trust and reliance grows, the company earns the opportunity to earn more revenue from each customer. Subscription companies grow revenue per customer by choosing the right pricing metric (what they charge for), creating upsell and cross-sell offers, and maybe even by raising prices. Some of the best subscription companies earn an average of 40% more year-on-year from their existing customers. That's 40% growth before accounting for any new customers!

Investors Reward Subscriptions

Subscription companies receive higher valuations in the markets than their traditional counterparts. They achieve between 4 and 10 times higher multiples of revenue. For any company raising money or in the public markets, this is *huge*. At the time of this writing (early 2020), Zoom has a market cap to revenue ratio of 40, and they aren't even profitable. Cisco's ratio is 4. Procter and Gamble's is 4.6.

Investors love subscription businesses because the revenue and growth are predictable and smooth. As we saw previously, subscription businesses can often account for 70% of a year's revenue goal on the first day of the year.

Yes, subscription companies have some fantastic advantages, but they also have one huge **disadvantage: cash flow**. When a traditional business lands a new customer, they get all of

70% of Annual Revenue on Day 1?

It's just math. At the end of the year, you can calculate how much revenue came from retention (meaning revenue from customers last year who stay subscribed). Here are two scenarios in which 70% of revenue can come from retention:

- If you win no new customers during the entire year and none of your customers decide to buy more than they did last year (both unlikely), you can churn 5.5% of your customers per month and still generate 70% of the previous year's revenue.

- If you have no churn at all, win no new customers during the year, their money upfront. In subscription businesses, it's common to get about $1/36^{th}$ per month. (This is NOT a recommendation. It's just a common business tactic.) In this case, it takes three years before they receive the same amount of revenue as a traditional business. This is extra painful when launching new products because all of the initial sales are from new customers. These companies are now only receiving incremental payments when they used to receive lump sums. This one fact can make the transition from a traditional business model to a subscription extremely painful, especially for CFOs.

and grow the revenue from your existing customers by 5.5% per month, then 70% of the revenue was due to retention, and the rest from expansion.

Of course, the reality will probably be somewhere between these extremes. For example, 20% annual growth and 2.5% monthly churn also implies 70% of the revenue was from retention. In chapter 7, you will learn the Subscription Growth Calculator, a tool that can do these calculations and much more.

Impactful Insight

Subscription businesses grow faster, have higher customer lifetime value, and higher valuations. Customers love them too.

As long as companies can support themselves financially through the cash flow crunch, the subscription business model is much better than the alternative. Sellers love them. Buyers love them. Investors love them. Subscriptions are awesome!

You were probably already convinced to create or transition to a subscription business, so let's jump into the details that matter. The next three chapters will provide frameworks and clarity to concepts you may understand intuitively. Yet, even subscription "experts" often find incredible value in the insight these explanations offer.

Summary

The subscription business model is rapidly growing in popularity because it's a positive transition for both buyers and sellers. Buyers love that they're more confident they'll receive the benefits they seek. The products tend to be simpler, easier to use, and more effective. They like the lower risk of the initial decision and the ability to use more of the product if and when they need to.

Sellers like the faster revenue growth that comes from subscriptions. They appreciate the higher lifetime value of their customers. Most of all, they love the higher valuations they get from investors and the stock market.

EXERCISE 1

Compare your current or future subscription-based product with a traditional product. What are the advantages and disadvantages to your company? To your customers?

2

Revenue Buckets

———————◆———————

Once you know subscriptions well, what you are about to read will become second nature. Even if you already run a subscription business, don't skip this chapter. It may feel like a review of concepts you've seen before, but this chapter will clarify how to prioritize, evaluate, and communicate more effectively in your company.

I had the pleasure of teaching an ISP (Internet Service Provider). They have been selling subscriptions longer than I have been alive, a fact that made me nervous that I had anything to teach them. Yet, when class was over, many attendees were thrilled with the clarity, simplicity and insights that came from this framework. Please don't skip this.

Traditional Business

To begin, let's take a look at the sales funnel of a traditional business. Above the funnel are many prospects (potential customers). These prospects are the responsibility of marketing, who strive to lead these candidates into the funnel by implementing campaigns and marketing messages. Once potential buyers are inside the company's funnel and have expressed enough interest, they move from 'prospects' to 'qualified leads.' This is when salespeople accept responsibility for concluding the sales process.

However, marketing remains involved by creating tools and messages to help salespeople sell more effectively. If you're in a business where you don't have direct salespeople, you can think of this as another step further along the buyer's journey. Different messages and tactics are required to convert potential buyers into customers. When marketing and sales have done their jobs well, a paying customer drops out of the bottom of the funnel. Woohoo! Does this sound familiar?

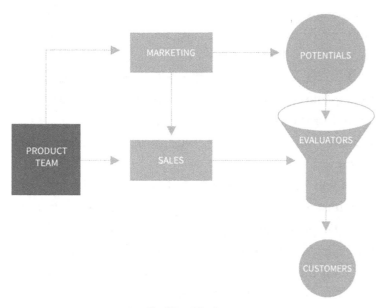

Traditional Business

How does a traditional business grow revenue? Simple: by investing more in marketing and sales. More marketing causes more prospects to enter the funnel. More sales investment brings more customers through the funnel and out of the bottom as brand new customers.

Subscription Business

This same process you just read about for traditional businesses also occurs in subscription businesses. However, in subscriptions, winning new customers is only a small portion of the company's overall revenue. In most cases, a new customer's first payment is much smaller than in a traditional business. If you have a subscription business, this means you just spent a lot of marketing and sales effort to win a tiny bit of revenue. Ouch. Is acquiring a customer worth the cost?

Of course, it is. There is a *lifetime value* to each customer, and your customer acquisition cost needs to be viewed in the context of how much a customer may pay you over time. This is why you invest in acquiring a new customer.

If you want to efficiently and rapidly grow a subscription business, you must manage three different revenue buckets: acquisition, retention, and expansion. You've likely heard these three terms before. I prefer to remove the consultant jargon and call them WIN, KEEP, and GROW. Acquisition means you need to WIN new customers. Retention means you have to KEEP your customers (so they keep paying you). And expansion means you have to GROW the amount of money any one customer pays you over time.

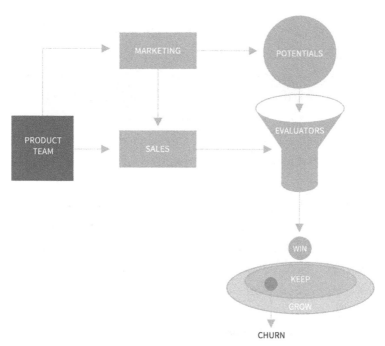

Subscription Business

The process of winning new customers is pretty much the same as in traditional businesses. The big difference is the value of the deal. In traditional companies, you mostly knew the contract's value when you signed it; you knew how much the customer would buy and what they'd pay you. In a subscription business, you don't know the deal's full value at the time of the sale. When you close the deal, you've only acquired the right to sell more to the customer. You must focus on delivering value to compel the customer to want to continue to pay you repeatedly, and eventually, even pay you more per month.

If you can't keep and grow customers, then winning customers is a losing proposition. You invest a lot of resources into winning customers, and you may not ever make it back if you don't keep and grow them. Ouch.

Pause, and think. As a subscription company, you need to WIN customers, KEEP customers, and GROW customers. How does this impact your current business model?

Seriously. If you didn't pause and think, do it now. These three words are not just a simplified articulation of what you may already know. They are the foundation of every strategy and tactic you should execute within your subscription business.

Impactful Insight

Managing a subscription is more complicated than a traditional business. You have to focus on winning, keeping, and growing customers.

WIN, KEEP, and GROW

This concept of WIN, KEEP, and GROW should drive how you choose to invest your resources.

Winning customers in a subscription business is a lot like winning them in a traditional business: you

At this point, you might be thinking, "didn't I buy a book about pricing? What does WIN, KEEP, and GROW have to do with pricing?" Fair question.

In my experience in pricing, a pricing problem is rarely about the price — the problem is almost always about value. Value is how much a buyer is willing to pay. Focusing on value thrusts us into a conversation about invest in marketing and sales. If you're in business, you already understand how to win customers.

Keeping customers is a critical goal in subscription businesses. When I first realized traditional companies don't really care if a buyer uses their product after the purchase, I was fascinated. As long as the buyer pays for it, doesn't return it, and doesn't complain too much, the seller is happy. But subscription companies can't do that. They need customers to use the product if they expect to optimize the lifetime value of those customers. Subscription companies do this in two ways: onboarding new customers and focusing on customer success to ensure customers continue to receive value.

how a buyer decides how much they are willing to pay.

Your pricing problem is not price; it's value.

We need to understand value, and we can only do this when we think about the decisions our buyers are making. In the context of WIN, KEEP, and GROW, here are three decisions buyers make concerning subscriptions:

WIN: should I buy from you or a competitor?

KEEP: should I continue to pay you for this product?

GROW: should I buy more from you?

In each of these decisions, the buyer has some perception of value. The key to pricing is giving them the product and messages to maximize their perception of value and setting a price slightly below that perception. It's not easy — and it's not even possible to do precisely. But making this your objective increases revenue and profit dollars. Isn't that why you focus on pricing and why you bought this book?

Once a subscription company wins a customer, they need to keep the customer. Subscribers keep paying while the subscription product delivers real value to the customer. Unfortunately, this doesn't always happen. Maybe the product would seem fantastic if only the customer knew how to use it. Hence, successful subscription companies often implement onboarding. These activities take a customer from introduction to proficiency. In the subscription industry, you often hear the phrase "time to value," meaning how long it takes a customer to go from the start (purchase) to receiving significant value. This book is not about onboarding, but the concept of helping new customers become successful is vital if you want to grow your subscription business.

Onboarding is often part of the Customer Success department, a new department created by subscription companies. Customer Success departments can take different forms. The great ones watch customers' usage patterns, determine what they are not doing well or maybe not doing at all, and then take actions to help the customer be more successful. Said differently, they help the customer get more value from the product. The more value a customer derives from a subscription, the less likely they are to unsubscribe.

You have to win a customer before you can keep one, and you have to keep one before you can grow the revenue you receive from one. You already know how to win customers — and you keep customers by onboarding them quickly, then by watching their usage behavior and proactively helping them get more and more value from your product. Next, you grow subscription payments from customers by pricing and packaging your products effectively, so the users who get the most value from your products willingly pay you more.

Using WIN, KEEP, GROW

Subscription businesses must manage all three of these revenue buckets — hopefully, you've internalized this point by now, or at least it is starting to grow on you. Specifically, there are two important ways you ought to think differently with this knowledge:

1. Every activity primarily focuses on one revenue bucket.
2. Every revenue bucket needs periodic focus.

Item 1 makes a ton of sense because almost every activity you undertake targets one of these three buckets. As some examples: A campaign to capture new customers targets WIN. Investing more in customer onboarding targets KEEP. And a promotion to get users to upgrade targets GROW. With few exceptions, your actions primarily impact one of the three revenue buckets. There may be some overlap, but there is likely a primary reason you choose to invest in any given activity. A great idea is to document which revenue bucket every task on your to-do list primarily targets.

Assigning activities to revenue buckets is the first step to prioritizing these actions. Your resources aren't infinite, and you'll often need to make economic decisions about how you should allocate them based on the relative importance of WIN, KEEP, or GROW.

Which leads to item 2. As your subscription moves through its product life cycle, the relative importance of WIN, KEEP, and GROW changes. You will want to change your mix of investments into each of these three revenue buckets over time.

Knowing which activities focus on which revenue buckets (item 1), you can more effectively manage the relative investments into the three revenue buckets (item 2).

Impactful Insight

WIN, KEEP, or GROW. Every Marketing tactic should focus on one of these but also consider the others.

Summary

The most fundamental difference between subscriptions and traditional products is the multiple revenue buckets you must manage for subscriptions: WIN, KEEP, and GROW. These revenue buckets should drive your thinking, your strategy, and your actions.

You need to optimize each revenue bucket based on your product's life cycle stage if you want to grow as quickly as possible.

Here are some other key insights from this chapter:

Limited cash flow is painful. Traditional businesses get a big chunk of money upfront when they win a customer. In contrast, subscription businesses get a bit of money upfront, and hopefully, monthly (or annual) payments after that. It typically takes three years for subscription companies to get the amount of cash equal to a single upfront payment.

Retention (KEEP) is crucial. Companies have to focus on how to keep their customers happy and paying. Otherwise, they never gain the same lifetime value as traditional businesses receive in an initial upfront payment. Usage matters: if somebody is not using the product, they will not pay for it month after month after month. (OK, maybe some people who belong to a gym pay month after month after month, just believing, or hoping, that someday they might use it.) But in most SaaS-type businesses, people who aren't using the product will churn out and stop paying. Losing them is painful.

Expansion (GROW) is usually under-emphasized. Most companies that go into subscriptions understand they have to win new customers *and* understand they have to keep their customers. But far too few focus enough on how to *grow* the revenue they receive from their current customers. Part 2 of the book discusses this in detail.

Subscription businesses are more complicated to manage than traditional businesses. You have to focus on winning, keeping, and growing customers, not *just* winning them. Every marketing tactic and new product feature should target one of these.

Zoom example

For many reasons, Zoom is one of my favorite subscription companies. Let's look at some examples of their marketing tactics to make some inferences about their actions toward WIN, KEEP, and GROW.

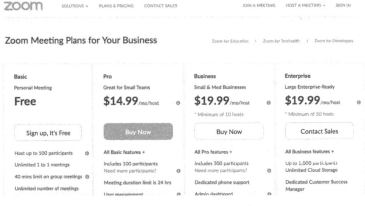

Zoom Pricing

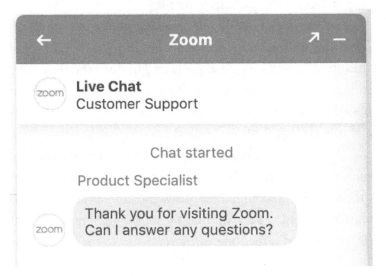

Zoom Chat Box

WIN: Zoom offers a free account. Anyone can sign up and use some of Zoom's features. Potential buyers can try it and see if it will work for them. Also, Zoom has a live chat box in the lower right-hand corner of their web page. If a shopper has questions, they can ask.

KEEP: I am a Zoom customer. When I first signed up, they sent several onboarding emails. "Have you tried this feature?" "Have you tried this use case?" "Here are some video resources so you can learn." They wanted me to become successful quickly. And even though I'm now a long-time customer, they still send tips and tricks in emails. They are sharing knowledge to make sure I'm as successful as I can be using Zoom.

GROW: The last bucket is growing customer revenue. Although we will go into more detail on these in chapter 8, here's a quick preview. If the user needs more capability, they can upgrade to Pro, Business, or even Enterprise. Zoom offers different versions of the product, such as a Webinar version. If the user likes the package they have but needs more "hosts," they can buy more. Zoom offers many ways to get subscribers to buy even more from them.

Zoom has created a set of tactics to win customers, keep customers, and grow customers. To develop a successful subscription business, you need to internalize this concept.

EXERCISE 2A

Study one or more subscription products you currently use. Look at their pricing pages and any emails you've received from them in the past. Take a piece of paper (or your iPad) and create a sheet with three columns. At the top of the columns, write WIN, KEEP, GROW. Now, articulate the tactics they seem to use for each of these three revenue buckets. What did you find?

EXERCISE 2B

You've now looked at what other companies do — but what are you doing? Go through everything in your to-do list and assign it to one of the three revenue buckets. Essentially, you are answering the question, why are we doing this project/task? The answer should be WIN, KEEP, or GROW.

Next, sort your projects and tasks by revenue bucket. Take a step back and evaluate. Which revenue buckets do you focus on primarily? Are any getting too much focus? Too little focus? If you're like most companies, you probably invest a lot of effort toward winning new customers, some effort spent keeping customers, and minimal effort growing revenue from current customers. You will learn more about why this happens in chapter 9, but for now, understand it's probably not optimal for your business. Unless you have a new subscription product in the market, you ignore one of the most impactful ways to grow your business.

3

Value Levers

———◆———

At last, we can get into pricing. You've internalized the foundational concept of subscription, and now it's time to play with pricing and value.

Fun fact — you are about to learn four pricing levers. Whether or not you are aware of them, you already use them. Even if you don't think about each one and make conscious decisions about them, you are already making implicit decisions about every one of them. You can't escape them; you can only attempt to manage them.

The four pricing levers are **price levels**, **market segments**, **pricing metrics**, and **packaging**. The price level is the only one directly tied to pricing — the other three tie to value. The price level is the number you choose to put on a product. Many pricing books, including my first book, Impact Pricing, help you think through this decision, so we won't dwell on it here. The essential price level decision is not unique to subscriptions; all companies have to choose a number as their price eventually. However, there are some nuances to subscription pricing — especially price changes. We discuss them in chapter 8.

The other three "pricing levers" are decisions that directly influence how much value you deliver to — and capture from — your market. Hence, we call these the three *value* levers: market segments, pricing metrics, and packaging. The remainder of this chapter focuses on these three value levers.

Each of the three value levers creates a substantial impact. The market segment you choose to serve will drive the features that go into your product, your marketing messages, and, ultimately, how much value you deliver to the market. The value you provide directly relates to the price you can charge, depending on whether or not your customers believe in the value, of course. Pricing metrics are the basis on which you monetize the customer's use of your product. In other words, what you charge for. Choose an effective one, and your company's revenue will grow as your customer's use of your product grows. Packaging determines how to bundle features into offers. Most SaaS companies use a version of Good, Better, Best, and for a good reason. Packaging may be the most challenging lever to get right, but the users who get the most value from your product will choose to buy more capabilities from you when done correctly.

Let's revisit the earlier statement that you use all of these levers, knowingly or not. Notice how you already made a market segment decision before you started reading this book. Even if you didn't make a *conscious* decision, you decided by default: you may be targeting everybody. You've also already decided on a pricing metric. What do you charge for? Many new subscription companies jump to charging per user, but often this is not the optimal pricing metric. What about your packaging? Are you offering Good, Better, Best options? Are you selling *everything* as an option? Whatever you are doing is a decision, even if you didn't make the decision consciously. Maybe what you are doing is working OK. However, you could drive even faster growth if you deliberately think through and make conscious decisions about your value levers.

If you already have a subscription offering, you may find it challenging to change any of these value levers. Changing any one of them requires a clear vision and leadership to execute change management in many parts of the company. After reading this book, you may decide it is worth your energy to lead a change management project. After all, big rewards only come to those who make big impacts.

Impactful Insight

Value levers are POWERFUL strategies; they affect many different departments. Use them, but use them carefully.

Market Segmentation

Most of us have a sense of what a market segment is, but it can be hard to define. Some people use industry or geography. Sometimes it's a specific role or size of a company. The truth is, any one of these definitions may work, but it may not.

I had the pleasure of teaching for Pragmatic Institute (Pragmatic Marketing at the time) for many years. They are by far the dominant trainer of product managers in the US. They define a market segment as "a group of companies or individuals with a common set of problems". Being a geek, I spent a lot of time thinking about whether their definition made sense, and I came to love it.

Why do businesses bother to define a market segment? The two most common reasons are to build better products and to create marketing messages targeted at a specific set of buyers. Both are great reasons. Both reasons are congruent with market problems. If a group of buyers all have the same set of problems, of course, you could build a product to solve their problems. You know which features to put in and which features to leave out. Then when it's time to market to them, you can simply say, "we solve your problems" while articulating what those problems are.

Let's say you're LinkedIn (another of my favorite subscription companies I often use as an example). Almost everybody in business wants to be able to find other people in an industry for some reason. Yet, LinkedIn said there are four sets of market problems or market segments. Recruiters need to find people to hire. Salespeople need to find people to buy from them. Job seekers need to find jobs. Everybody else is ... well, everybody else. But you can quickly see from the recruiter, salesperson, and job seeker categories, each segment has a common set of problems. LinkedIn created four different versions of products for these four market segments: Hiring, Sales, Career, and Business. LinkedIn has unique marketing messages for each market segment. I haven't found a more "pragmatic" way to define market segments than by their problems.

LinkedIn Market Segments

Although the two most common and apparent reasons for market segmentation are creating compelling products and creating useful marketing messages, there is also a third, powerful reason. Different market segments often have very different willingness to pay. When you make different products for different market segments, you can charge significantly different prices.

Willingness to Pay for LinkedIn by Market Segment
Research by Profitwell 2018

Reconsider the LinkedIn example. LinkedIn can (and does) create different products for the different segments and charges substantially different prices. It seems evident that recruiters can, and will, pay a lot more than a job seeker; accordingly, LinkedIn's recruiter product is much more expensive than their job seeker product.

One common question related to market segments is, how many market segments should you have? Well, you could have between one and an infinite number. Though true, this isn't helpful — so let's try to narrow it down a little. What if you didn't segment your market, and instead, you combine everybody into a single "segment"? Your product and your messaging lack impact. What if you chose a single customer and made them your market segment? Your product could be perfect for that customer, and your marketing might resonate immensely, but you'd be doing marketing and product development for only one buyer; each 'segment' would be minuscule.

The right answer is almost always somewhere between those two extremes. My recommendation, especially if you're starting, is to choose one market segment much smaller and more specific than feels comfortable to you. Most companies are afraid of losing business, but if they'd focus all of their resources on a smaller segment, they could progress more quickly. Once you prove a success, you can either expand that market segment or target an additional segment.

Focusing on market segments works so well because you genuinely understand what products each segment needs. You truly understand the problems you are solving for each segment, enabling you to communicate more impactfully with the people in it. And most importantly, you have a better understanding of the value you are delivering, so you can price more appropriately.

Pricing Metric

The second of our three value levers is a pricing metric. A pricing metric is how you charge for your products. Most companies selling physical products use units as the pricing metric. For example, McDonald's charges for hamburgers; the hamburger is their pricing metric. However, there are exceptions. Before giving you the exceptions, think about how you would sell tires, used books, coffee, or jet engines. Most of us would set a price for the tire, used book, cup of coffee, or the jet engine. But you don't have to. Michelin sells commercial truck tires by the mile. Some book markets in India sell used books by the kilogram. Some cafés in Europe sell coffee by the hour. GE sells jet engines by the hour. These examples are to encourage you to think beyond what seems obvious in your business regarding pricing metrics.

When Salesforce launched its software as a Service (SaaS) sales tool, they charged by the user. Since then, charging by the user has become the most common metric and thus has become the obvious choice for SaaS companies. However, in many cases, charging by the user may be sub-optimal.

Before choosing a pricing metric, you want to understand what *value metrics* your buyers use. A value metric is how your customers measure the value they receive. I often ask my clients to fill in the following blanks: "Our customers love our product because their _____ went from _____ to _____." The first blank is a key performance indicator (KPI). The second and third blanks are how they measure the KPI to show improvement. For example, "My customers love my training because their average discount rate went from 7% to 5%." Or, "My customers love my training because their average customer lifetime value increased from $1,200 to $1,500." There may be more than one relevant value metric, so think broadly.

Once you understand the value metric, you can choose a pricing metric highly correlated with the value metric. This may not be simple, but when implemented thoughtfully, it is incredible.

The power of a well-chosen pricing metric comes from capturing customer growth. A useful pricing metric automatically grows your revenue as your customers become more successful and use more of your product. For example, if a Salesforce customer grows to double their original size, they probably also double the number of people on their sales team. Since Salesforce charges by the user, Salesforce doubled their revenue without any additional effort. PayPal charges a percentage of the transaction. Constant Contact® charges by the number of emails a customer sends out. Atlassian offers JIRA at a low price for small teams, then ramps up the pricing as team size grows. In each of these cases, the more someone uses the product, the more value they receive, and the more they pay. All is good in the world.

As we've seen, pricing metrics are *hugely* valuable. They are powerful tools and can influence your revenue and your growth rate dramatically. Choose wisely. Choose intentionally.

Packaging

The last of our three value levers is packaging. Your company has created a ton of features and capabilities. Packaging is the act of defining how to combine these into attractive offers for your market segments.

There are several kinds of packaging techniques:

All you can eat packaging is one price for everything. It's like going to a buffet. You pay the price to get in and then gorge yourself. Amazon Prime and Peleton are two examples of 'all you can eat' pricing.

A la carte pricing means offering almost everything as an option. You can also think of this as 'design your own' or 'build your own.' When you order a pizza, you can order any toppings you'd like. This is 'a la carte' pricing. GoDaddy's offerings use this technique.

Upfront payments are when the buyer pays a large sum at the beginning of the relationship and pays smaller amounts periodically after. Gym memberships tend to require an initiation fee. Gyms do this to get buy-in and commitment since buyers are less likely to drop out if they paid the up-front fee. Technology companies tend to use upfront payments to ensure they cover their costs. Those who have high implementation costs or hardware products (think the Internet of Things) often want to make sure their hard costs are covered.

Creating different *versions of your product for different market segments* is an effective packaging technique, as we saw in the section on market segments. LinkedIn does this. So do ZipCar, Zoom, and many others.

By far, the most powerful and most common technique is *Good/Better/Best* packaging. This technique has many advantages: it makes it easier for buyers to decide to buy, and it provides an upgrade path for growing customers. To see some excellent examples, visit some SaaS pricing pages; almost all of them have at least three columns: good, better, and best.

Options are those extras some buyers want to buy. The expectation is a buyer will buy the base product and then choose to purchase one or more additional options. Popcorn at the movie theater is an option. You buy the base product — the movie — and then decide if you will buy the option (popcorn). Options are a prevalent technique in SaaS but not always apparent on their pricing pages. For LinkedIn, you could buy more InMails. For Zoom, you could buy their Webinar option. For TurboTax, you could buy their California State option.

Options should be valuable features to a sub-segment of your market segment and should be priced relatively high. You don't want to manage numerous low-priced options. When deciding whether to make a feature a paid option, you should consider any overheads incurred by treating the feature as an option, customer expectations, and the competitive landscape. For example, if only a few customers are likely to buy the option, the limited revenue it generates may not be worth the complexity and overhead it creates. Or, if most of your customers need the feature, your competitors include it in their standard offering, and you charge for it, then customers will be turned off. Thus, there's a range of demand (perhaps 20-50% of customers) in which packaging a feature as an option may make sense.

The best packaging is almost always a combination of the last two mentioned. Create Good/Better/Best offerings, plus options targeted at specific market segments. This packaging is what LinkedIn does. By now, you know they have a product offering targeting recruiters, and you know recruiters would pay more than job seekers. Here's an obvious question: Do all recruiters have the same willingness to pay for LinkedIn? The answer, of course, is "no." That's why LinkedIn offers Good/Better/Best products targeted directly at recruiters. These Good/Better/Best products are different than what you would get in the salesperson's packages. They are targeted at — and within — a market segment.

Impactful Insight

Every company uses all three value metrics: Market segmentation, pricing metric, and packaging. Great companies use them intentionally and thoughtfully.

The Interconnections

Throughout this book, we often talk about the three value levers as if they were independent decisions; but surely, you've already realized they are not. We talked about using good, better, best packaging within a market segment in the packaging section, so clearly, market segments and packaging are closely related.

Packaging is also closely related to the pricing metric. It is quite possible to find an excellent pricing metric, like InMails for LinkedIn. Then, like LinkedIn, instead of charging for each individual InMail, they bundle them up. They put 10 in the good package, 20 in the better package, and 30 in the best package. They use the pricing metric strategically inside their packaging.

Finally, pricing metrics can be different for different market segments. LinkedIn uses InMails as a pricing metric for job seekers and salespeople. They use Jobs Posted as a metric for recruiters.

Not only are the three value levers interconnected with each other, but they impact many departments and roles inside a company. Each one is complicated, and many people inside the company have strong often inflexible opinions. It is highly unlikely you can just say, "change the pricing metric to usage-based," and watch it happen — even if you're the CEO. It takes teamwork and collaboration. Don't let this discourage you; the potential positive impact should motivate you to want to lead the change — but know this — changing any of these is *not* easy.

The challenge of changing these also emphasizes the importance of starting on the right foot. Maybe you want to start out charging by the user because it's intuitive, it's easy to implement, and buyers seem to accept it. Or, maybe you want to launch your subscription with a usage-based pricing metric, so you don't have to change it later. I advise you to make this strategic decision intentionally, which you can only do *after* you've thought through many of the optimal pricing metrics.

Whether you decide intentionally or not, you do decide. Every company targets a market segment, even if the segment is everybody. Every company has chosen one or more pricing metrics; it is the item they put on the invoice or receipt. Every company sells its products in some type of packaging. They can't escape it.

Choosing the right market segment(s) can accelerate your success. Choosing the right pricing metric(s) enables your company to grow as your customers grow. Building effective packaging incentivizes trial, adoption, and even upgrades. Wouldn't your company be better off if you made these decisions with forethought and serious consideration?

Value levers are powerful tools. You have to make these decisions, so make the decisions intentionally, not by default.

Summary

In this chapter, you learned you have four levers to influence pricing. The first one is the price you charge. The other three levers are value levers, decisions your company makes to affect the amount of value you can capture from your market.

A well-chosen market segment enables you to develop more impactful products and marketing messages. A useful pricing metric causes your revenue to grow as your customers receive more value from your product. Packaging, done well, provides a critical opportunity for you to gain more revenue from your customers as they learn more about what your product does.

Although we treat these three levels individually, they often work in concert. When done exceptionally well, the growth of a subscription product can be exponential.

Zoom Example

Zoom provides an excellent example of using all three value levers.

The first value lever we'll consider is the market segment. What you can see in Figure X below is the menu you see when you click 'Solutions' on the home page of the Zoom website. Under Industries, they've broken this down into different market segments. Each one of these industries probably has other jargon, and Zoom is communicating to each of them with a different set of criteria or values that concern them.

zoom SOLUTIONS ▾ PLANS & PRICING CONTACT SALES	JOIN A MEETING HOST
PRODUCTS	**INDUSTRIES**
Meetings and Chat HD video, audio, collaboration & chat	**Education** Expand traditional classrooms in the cloud
Rooms and Workspaces Power up your conference rooms with video	**Finance** Improve customer experiences & communications
Phone System Enterprise cloud phone system	**Government** Increase productivity & engagement for all agencies
Video Webinars Full-featured, easy-to-use, engaging webinars	**Healthcare** HIPAA-compliant telehealth technology & workflows
App Marketplace Integrations and bots to use with Zoom	

Zoom Market Segments

Let's now look at pricing metrics. Next to the prices, we see they're charging per month per host. So, you could say the pricing metric is both per month and per host. Notice, however, they have another, less obvious pricing metric: maximum participants. In the Pro version, you can have 100 participants; in the Business version, you can have up to 300. In the Enterprise version, you can have up to 500, and with Enterprise Plus, you can have 1000 participants.

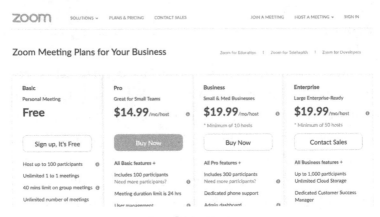

Zoom Pricing Metrics

What's fascinating is they have two different mechanisms for their pricing metrics. The metric next to the price is on a per-unit basis: every time you add a new host, you pay them another $19.99. In contrast, they priced the total number of participants in tiers, so if you need to accommodate more than 300 participants, you have to make a quantum leap to 500 or 1000, rather than buying capacity for just a few more. This tiered structure motivates their customers to use more of their product; when customers have access to more of a resource, they tend to use more of it (just like storage space in your house.)

The last of our three value levers is packaging. It's pretty apparent Zoom has Good/Better/Best offerings, and they also have a Free option to get a lot of people familiar with the product. Additionally, some companies will list a premium version at the very high end, with "Call Us" rather than listing a price. Zoom has created its packaging with the plan of getting you to sign up for the free package, then upselling you to Pro once you need more capability. Ideally, you're adding more hosts as your company grows, but you may also need more functionality, so you'll upgrade to the Business level. You can see how Zoom is using Good/Better/Best strategically and how they also offer add-on options with each plan. For example, if you need more than 100 participants but don't want to upgrade from Pro to business, one choice is to buy more participants from the a la carte option.

EXERCISE 3A

Look at other subscription companies. If you dig deeper into the best companies, you will see all three value levers. Look to see who they target; do they approach different market segments differently, or are they targeting everybody? What pricing metrics do they use? Observe what they do for packaging. As you look at several of your favorite subscription companies, you'll learn to quickly and easily spot their decisions. If you encounter any that don't seem to make sense, remember legacy decisions may have imposed constraints preventing the company from choosing a strategy they might have used if they were starting anew.

EXERCISE 3B

Follow the steps in Exercise 3A for your own product. How are you currently using the value levers? What market segment have you defined? What pricing metrics are you using? And lastly, how are you packaging your products? At this point, don't judge them as good or bad; just identify them.

4

Unit Metrics

———————◆———————

When running a subscription business, you need to track different metrics than you do for a traditional business. Although traditional companies don't call them "unit metrics," they do track unit metrics. For each order, you know the revenue (R) of the order and the Cost of Goods Sold (COGS), from which you can calculate your profit margin (R - COGS)/R. You also know the average cost of sales and any other allocated overhead costs. With all of this, you can calculate the profitability of each sale. This explanation might not be precisely accurate in all companies, but it's a reasonable representation.

You cannot calculate the same unit metrics in a subscription business because you don't know the revenue of any given sale. You don't know how many months any subscriber will stay — especially when they first subscribe

— so you don't know how much they will pay you. Hence, if you want to calculate the profitability of any sale, you need a different set of metrics. Instead of looking at actual revenue and profit, you'll be looking at the expected profit.

Monitoring these metrics is crucial to managing your subscription business well. Earlier, you learned you need to WIN, KEEP, and GROW customers in subscriptions. Knowing your metrics will help you identify when something is not right with one of these revenue buckets.

This chapter covers the basic unit metrics. In the next section of the book, you will learn some additional metrics to monitor your product life cycle in different phases, but they all start with these five basic metrics.

The five basic unit metrics are:

- customer acquisition cost (CAC)
- monthly recurring revenue (MRR)
- MRR churn rate
- average revenue per subscriber (ARPS)
- lifetime value of your customer (LTV)

Sometimes you will see annual numbers instead of monthly numbers. As a general rule, you will want to use monthly metrics to manage your business and yearly metrics for reporting purposes. The annual numbers are less volatile, but they are too long-term to notify you of pending trouble.

As we go through these unit metrics, we will refer back to how they relate to our three revenue buckets: WIN,

KEEP, and GROW. You will want to monitor those revenue buckets separately.

Customer Acquisition Cost — CAC

The total cost of acquiring a customer includes sales and marketing expenses. Define a period, usually a month, and sum up all of the marketing and sales expenses in that period. Then divide that sum by the number of new customers you gained in the same period.

In reality, the sales and marketing resources invested in one month may not yield paying customers until a later month. Still, the metric assumes the same month, which works as long as the investment and the win rate are relatively consistent. Besides, if you are growing investment in sales and marketing, it will make CAC look higher, which is relevant for a critical metric coming up in chapter 5.

You may have already realized an exceptionally good or bad month (in terms of new customers) would mess up this metric. If you have spikes in customer acquisition, you can extend the period. For example, you may want to use a quarter or even a year to stabilize the result. The key is to use the same period for your expenses *and* the count of new customers. The disadvantage of a more extended period is it doesn't reveal improvements in sales and marketing techniques as you learn to be more effective.

Applying this to revenue buckets, CAC is the expense side of the WIN bucket. It is not relevant to KEEP or GROW.

Monthly Recurring Revenue — MRR

Your MRR is simply the total revenue you received for your subscription products in any given month. It only includes recurring revenue, not any one-time payments like purchases of hardware or implementation services.

Although MRR is backward-looking, it also can project forward. Since it is recurring, you can reasonably expect to get a substantial percentage of last month's revenue again next month if you keep your customers satisfied. You won't get all of it due to churn, but you should ignore churn when calculating the MRR metric. We account for churn next.

You will sometimes see ARR, Annual Recurring Revenue. As a rule of thumb, companies use MRR to manage their business and ARR to report results.

Now, look at how this metric applies to revenue buckets. MRR minus churn is the KEEP bucket. As you win or grow customers, MRR goes up; MRR is the baseline if you keep all customers and don't win or grow additional ones.

MRR Churn Rate

Churn happens when subscribers unsubscribe — they leave us. The metrics for churn could be in either subscribers or dollars. Churn in subscribers means counting how many left us. Churn in dollars comes from adding up the revenue we lost *because* those subscribers left us. Churn in dollars is also the amount of MRR we will not get the following month. Both of those churn metrics are absolute numbers; we are more interested in the relative numbers.

For the MRR churn rate, take the churn in dollars of one month divided by the MRR of the previous month. This calculation yields a percentage.

For example, assume we received $100,000 MRR in September from 1000 customers. In October, 20 of those subscribers didn't renew. In total, those 20 customers paid us $1,500 in September, revenue we didn't receive in October.

Churn in subscribers = 20

Churn in dollars = $1,500

Monthly churn rate = $1,500/$100,000 = 1.5%

Note that October's MRR may be higher than $100,000 due to winning new customers. For example, if we win 40 new customers at $3,000 for the month, October's MRR would be $101,500 ($100,000 - $1,500 + $3,000). For calculating MRR Churn Rate do not include revenue from the Win or Grow buckets of the current period.

We call these unit metrics because we calculate (estimating) what is happening with customers, not just overall revenue. We want to know how much of our revenue came from the customers we had last month, and how much came from winning new customers. These are the WIN and KEEP revenue buckets. MRR churn rate is a measure of how well you maintain revenue in the KEEP bucket.

Average Revenue Per Subscriber — ARPS

To calculate ARPS, simply divide MRR by the number of customers. You will use this number to calculate lifetime value — a crucial metric in managing subscriptions.

Sometimes, instead of ARPS, you will see average revenue per user (ARPU). This modification may come in handy when you sell to large companies, and they have many users. For example, Slack may have a contract with a large customer like Facebook. Facebook may be the one subscriber, but they have many users. Use common sense when determining what to use as the denominator of this metric. The key here is whatever you use is what you will use for deciding customer acquisition cost and lifetime value. You may even want to try several different denominators and think about which one gives you the most meaningful metrics to track.

Applying this to revenue buckets, ARPS uses a combination of the KEEP and GROW buckets.

Lifetime Value — LTV

Now we get to the magic metric: lifetime value. (Some people call this CLV for Customer Lifetime Value). In a traditional business, when you get an order, you know the value of the order. When you get an order in a subscription business, you can only calculate the *likely* value of the order. This uncertainty is where lifetime value comes in.

Lifetime value = ARPS * GM% / MRR Churn rate. GM% here is your gross margin percentage. For many SaaS companies, GM% is so close to 100% you can ignore it. However, if you have significant variable or incremental costs to serve your subscribers, you will want to include it.

Applying this to revenue buckets — because ARPS is for KEEP and GROW, so is LTV.

Reported Results		
Recurring revenue month prior	$	30,000
Recurring revenue	$	35,000
Gross margin		70%
Subscribers		1,000
New subscribers		100
Average Revenue per New Subscriber	$	10
Subscribers churned		12
Total revenue churned	$	750
Cost of sales	$	20,000
Marketing	$	15,000
Unit Metrics		
CAC	$	350
MRR	$	35,000
MRR Churn Rate		2.5%
ARPS	$	35
LTV	$	980

Example of Unit Metrics

Many of these KPIs may be reported to you by your company's finance department.

There are probably hundreds of metrics or KPI's you could choose to use

Let's say your accounting department gave you the reported results in the example shown above. Let's use the formulas to determine these Unit Metrics.

CAC or Customer Acquisition Cost starts with the total spending on in your subscription business. You've probably heard, "what gets measured, gets managed." The problem with too many metrics is it isn't apparent which ones are key. These unit metrics are a fantastic start. I always recommend you begin with these metrics and then slowly add more as you find a specific need.

Trends

Once you get in the habit of calculating these metrics, start looking for trends, and track them over time. Are they moving

sales and marketing, $35,000 ($20,000+$15,000). Divide this by the 100 new subscribers to get $350. MRR is provided by accounting. Additional calculations should not be needed.

MRR Churn rate is the total revenue churned ($750) divided by MRR — revenue the month prior ($30,000) — to yield .025, which is 2.5%.

ARPS or Average Revenue Per Subscriber is simply MRR ($35,000) divided by the total number of subscribers (1000), which is $35.

LTV or Lifetime Value is ARPS ($35) divided by MRR Churn rate (.025) times Gross margin (.70), resulting in $980.

in the direction you expect? Can you explain the reasons they are moving? Below are some possible explanations you might consider if the numbers start trending in the wrong direction.

If your CAC is going up, you may be targeting new market segments that aren't as good a fit. You may have already found the low hanging fruit, and now your sales team has to work harder to win deals.

If MRR is going down, you have a significant problem. It probably means you are losing customers faster than you are winning them. You need to focus on retention. MRR rarely goes down but do watch to see if it grows as quickly as you expect.

If the MRR churn rate is going up, your customer success team may be doing something wrong. You also may be winning more customers that are not a good fit.

If ARPS is going down, it means you are bringing in newer, smaller customers, or maybe your current customers are using less or downgrading, so they pay you less.

If LTV is going down, there are many possible causes. For example, it could be the type of new customers you are winning or problems with retention.

The whole point of watching the trends is to detect when something is going wrong to fix it and see whether what you are doing is working well.

Cohorts

The above unit metrics provide keen insight into your overall business. However, you can glean even more incredible insights when you calculate all of them for cohorts.

A cohort is a group of customers with something in common you want to track. For example, you may have a cohort of customers who bought during a specific promotion. Do they have longer or shorter LTV? How does this compare to the CAC?

You can make any group of customers a cohort, but you want to do it for a purpose. The goal is to compare one cohort to other cohorts or the overall average. Using cohort analytics is how you track the effectiveness of your marketing programs, products, and other business decisions.

For example, do you want to know how valuable a trade show was? Let's assume you can track the deals closed from the leads captured at the trade show. In a traditional business, you know the value of your closed sales — but it's not so easy for subscriptions. What if the subscribers who purchased from a trade show churn more quickly or more slowly than a typical subscriber? You can work this out by grouping those who purchased due to the trade show into a cohort to calculate their lifetime value.

Another beneficial use of cohorts is to track the responses of different market segments. Instead of looking at the overall company numbers, look at the results by market segment to inform you which segment(s) are the most profitable.

The good news is, you don't have to pre-define a cohort before you collect data. Once you have the data for each customer, you can mix and match customers into different cohorts to test different results. Any single customer can belong to more than one cohort. For example, one customer may go in the 2020 cohort, the trade show cohort, the "downloaded the trial" cohort, and the international cohort. The idea is to combine customers for a purpose and to track their performance. When you find that specific actions lead to higher LTV and lower CAC, you can identify the underlying reasons why these are effective and take more of these actions.

Unit metrics are the basis for monitoring and managing your overall subscription business. Cohorts carve up the aggregate data into useful subsets to provide data-driven insights.

Impactful Insight

Know your unit metrics. Track their trends. Look at them by cohort.

Summary

It's essential to choose the right metrics for your subscription business. The critical problem with subscription metrics is you can't know the value of an order when you get one — you must estimate it.

The five unit metrics described in this chapter are tried and true in subscription companies around the world. Start with these, then add more metrics if you find you need to.

You also want to watch your unit metrics' trends, both on their own and by cohort. The trends show you what is and isn't working inside your subscription business.

EXERCISE 4A

Hand-calculate the unit metrics and the WIN, KEEP, GROW revenue for this data set. The answers are available on the next page.

Reported Results		
Recurring revenue month prior	$	480,000
Recurring revenue	$	500,000
Gross margin		60%
Subscribers		10,000
New subscribers		200
Average Revenue per New Subscriber	$	100
Subscribers churned		30
Total revenue churned	$	5,000
Cost of sales	$	400,000
Marketing	$	100,000
Win Keep Grow		
Win		
Keep		
Grow		
Unit Metrics		
CAC		
MRR		
MRR Churn Rate		
ARPS		
LTV		

Exercise 4A

EXERCISE 4B

If you currently have a subscription business, find or calculate each of these unit metrics for your product.

Win Keep Grow	
Win	
Keep	
Grow	
Unit Metrics	
CAC	
MRR	
MRR Churn Rate	
ARPS	
LTV	

Exercise 4B

Reported Results		
Recurring revenue month prior	$	480,000
Recurring revenue	$	500,000
Gross margin		60%
Subscribers		10,000
New subscribers		200
Average Revenue per New Subscriber	$	100
Subscribers churned		30
Total revenue churned	$	5,000
Cost of sales	$	400,000
Marketing	$	100,000
Win Keep Grow		
Win	$	20,000
Keep	$	475,000
Grow	$	5,000
Unit Metrics		
CAC	$	2,500
MRR	$	500,000
MRR Churn Rate		1.04%
ARPS	$	50.00
LTV	$	2,880
LTV/CAC		1.152

Exercise 4A Answers

Section 2.

Subscription Lifecycle

Just like products have lifecycles, so do subscriptions. When you first launch a subscription, you need to focus on getting it off the ground. This means finding customers and ensuring they are happy with your subscription. This initial tweaking of your product and marketing is finding your product-market fit. It's not easy, but it is essential. After you figure it out, your subscription grows. Eventually, you will have many subscribers, and the pool of non-subscribers or potential customers dwindles. Then your efforts need to shift toward growing the revenue you earn from current customers. This transition represents the lifecycle of a subscription.

The best way to think about this is the shifting importance of the three main revenue buckets (WIN, KEEP, and GROW). Early-stage products must focus heavily on winning and keeping customers. They need to know if the customers they are winning are profitable and how profitable they are. Growing companies don't stop winning or keeping customers, but they often find even more rapid growth, and more profit comes from adding efforts to increase revenue from current customers. Mature companies shift even more resources into the GROW bucket as there are fewer and fewer new customers to win.

Different metrics are more valuable at different times in a subscription product's lifecycle. Specifically, very early subscriptions must focus on the viability metric, while more mature subscriptions need to start watching net dollar retention. The next two chapters discuss these metrics. The subsequent chapters in this section help you understand what actions you should take based on your subscription's lifecycle stage.

5

Early Stage Subscriptions

———————◆———————

Viability Metric

The viability metric is used by investors to see if a startup has established a product-market-price fit. Even if you're not looking for investment, you want to know you have product-market-price fit before investing in growth. To calculate it, simply divide LTV by CAC. The rule of thumb investors use to determine an effective product-market-price fit is LTV/CAC >3; in other words, a subscription business must earn at least three times as much money from a customer as it costs to acquire a customer. Three may seem higher than you'd expect; let's see why it makes sense.

First, think about a traditional business selling expensive hardware. Each product has real COGS (cost of goods sold). Price minus COGS is gross margin, or how much the company makes for selling the product before taking business overhead into account. The company can also determine the cost of sales, reasonably estimated by finance. What if the cost of selling a product is higher than the gross margin? The company loses money. The gross margin must be much higher than the cost of sales to cover the company's overhead *and* generate a profit.

Now, think about a subscription. If you have a sales (and marketing) cost, how do you know if you're profitable? Assume you are selling a SaaS product where the COGS are close to 0. This means revenue and gross margin are nearly equal. So, if you close a deal for $100 per month, but it costs you $500 to win a customer, are you profitable? It depends on how many months the customer pays you.

This is where LTV shines. How long will a customer continue to pay $100 per month? If you calculate the average lifetime of a customer to find it is eight months, and you spent $500 to acquire $800 in revenue, then your viability metric is $800/$500=1.6. Not horrible, but not yet enough to make investors happy. A viability metric of 1.6 implies you cover your CACs and pay some of your overhead, but there probably isn't enough money for profit or investment in growth.

Even if you are not looking for funding, you should be thinking along these same lines. Can you get your viability metric over three? This will indicate you have the potential to grow rapidly.

HubSpot case study

Let's look at a case study about Hubspot. You can see their numbers in the figure below. They had a CAC of around $6,025 and a customer LTV of over $10,000. Since LTV was greater than CAC, they went to their board for permission to invest significantly more in SEO, sales, and marketing. The board said, "Whoa! You're not that viable. You need to get the LTV/CAC greater than three first." OK, I'm pretty sure those weren't the exact words, but you get the idea.

CAC	ARPS	MRR churn rate	MARGIN	LTV	LTV/CAC
$6,025	$429	3.5%	83%	$10,074	1.67

Q1 2011

Hubspot Unit Metrics

There are two ways to increase the viability metric: increase LTV or decrease CAC. But it's not enough just to say you want to change those numbers. How do you do it? In HubSpot's case, they decided to focus on a narrower market segment — probably a smart decision for many businesses.

Focusing on a market segment enabled them to lower CAC by knowing and communicating targeted messages to resonate clearly with that segment. They can focus their marketing and sales efforts on the clients they know will value their product the most, and in doing so, increase LTV. Their customers will buy more, pay more, *and* stay longer.

HubSpot decided to focus on larger, high-end customers. They shifted the resources they were investing to win small customers to win larger customers instead; a year later, their unit metrics changed dramatically. Their CAC actually went up. Because they were going after larger customers, they spent more to win fewer customers. However, because they were going after bigger customers, their ARPS went up too. Churn decreased, which often happens when you win bigger customers. They are harder to win, but once you win them, they don't change their minds easily. With higher ARPS and lower churn, their LTV skyrocketed from 10,000 to 23,000. Wow. Their viability metric went from 1.67 to 3.5.

CAC	ARPS	MRR churn rate	MARGIN	LTV	LTV/CAC
$6,025	$429	3.5%	83%	$10,074	1.67
←			Q1 2011		→
$6,880	$583	2%	81%	$23,775	3.5
←			Q1 2012		→

Hubspot Unit Metrics A Year Later

In 2011, they needed to spend $6,000 to win a customer worth $10,000. This certainly isn't a large margin, and the revenue comes in over many months, not immediately. It feels risky. In 2012, they needed to spend $7,000 to win a customer worth $24,000. Now *that's* profitability.

Improving the viability metric demonstrates an improving product-market-price fit. In other words, they found an excellent solution to a problem the market has and found buyers who are willing to pay for it.

Getting your viability metric greater than three isn't a hard-and-fast rule. However, every investor who writes about this topic uses three as the benchmark. Given the HubSpot example, you can see how it makes sense for you to adopt this as a rule. If you get to 2.9, you're probably fine. But over time, by improving your product and becoming more efficient with sales and marketing, the number should continue to climb.

Timing of Actions

Now let's relate viability to your WIN, KEEP, and GROW revenue buckets. When your viability metric is less than three, here's what you should do for each of your buckets:

WIN: Don't invest heavily in anything. Instead, you should be tweaking your product, techniques, market segments, and pricing to win the right customers effectively.

KEEP: Tweak your onboarding and customer success programs to keep customers for as long as possible. Find out what compels users to churn. The best way to understand why they unsubscribe is to call them; ask them about their experience. Listen.

GROW: Completely ignore this bucket. It is a waste of your time this early in your product lifecycle. If you don't have many customers, don't waste your resources trying to grow revenue from the few you do have.

To summarize, when viability is less than three, you should first focus on product-market-price fit. Do you have the right product? Have you found the right customers? Are you using the right pricing model and levels? Tweak and test. The goal is to prove product-market-fit by attaining a viability metric above 3.

Once the viability metric is over three, it is now time to scale your business. Here's what you should do for each of the three revenue buckets once your viability metric is three or higher:

WIN: Invest significantly in sales and marketing to acquire new customers quickly.

KEEP: Put programs in place for onboarding and customer success to retain these newly acquired customers. You're just doing what you already know how to do but at scale.

GROW: Move slowly. When viability first exceeds three, continue to ignore expansion initially. After you've built a healthy user base, you will begin to shift some focus to growing customers. The sad truth is many subscription companies never think about growing their customers. I'll say more about this in chapter 9.

To summarize, when viability first exceeds three, focus on scaling what you have. Invest and grow as quickly as you can. After you've built a business with many users, you will begin to work on growing revenue from your customers.

Impactful Insight
Your viability metric drives the prioritization of your early-stage tactics.

Viability of Cohorts

Let's say you have a successful subscription product. The viability metric exceeds 3 by a lot. You have ramped up growth in your market segment and are doing well. You're thinking, "maybe it's time to expand into another market segment." Excellent!

Keep track of your unit metrics for the new market segment — this is simply a cohort of customers. Enter the new segment cautiously, calculate and monitor the viability metric for this cohort, and once it exceeds 3 it's time to ramp your efforts into this segment.

You can and should do this same thing for many cohorts. Do you want to expand internationally? Do you want to attend a new trade show? Do you want to try a new distribution technique? Each of these could be considered a cohort. Enter them slowly, monitor the cohort's viability metric, and wait for it to exceed 3 before trying to scale.

Other Metrics

So far, you've read about the basic unit metrics. There are many more metrics you could be using. The problem with metrics is that what gets measured gets managed. The approach I recommend is to start with the metrics you've already learned. Then, as you decide you need more focus in a specific area, choose another metric or two to help you target a particular goal. You will find it logical to break metrics up into the three revenue buckets (WIN, KEEP, and GROW). Below are several you may choose to use. Just don't add too many, and only add one when it helps you achieve a stated objective.

WIN

When you want to improve your win/revenue bucket, you have several metrics you could be watching.

Conversions — Companies typically measure conversions based on the number of people who purchase as a percentage of the number of people who visited the purchase page. You could do other conversion rates, such as the number who see the purchase page as a percentage of the number visiting the website. The idea is, once you identify the typical buyer's journey for your customers, you can track the conversions along that route.

Net New MRR is the MRR you won from new subscribers. Tracking this as a trend is helpful to make sure you are improving. Following it as a percentage of total MRR will show you when you need to focus on other revenue buckets because this percentage will inevitably decrease over time. When you first start, 100% of your revenue in the first month is Net New MRR. If you book the same Net New MRR the second month and don't churn any customers, then the second month's Net New MRR makes up 50% of your total revenue (first month plus the second month). In the third month, it goes to 33%. Of course, it is never that clean, but you get the idea.

New Subscribers — You can track the number of new subscribers you win. This is especially helpful when new subscribers start with a much lower average revenue than the ARPS, Average Revenue Per Subscriber. This lets you know the pipeline is filling up, and you may be confident the revenue the new subscribers pay will grow over time.

ARPNS stands for average revenue per NEW subscriber. Watching this as a trend shows you how your initial offers and sales teams are doing. If you choose to go after different segments, you will likely find this number different for each segment.

ACV is the average contract value. Here you are taking into account all of the contract's revenue, including one-time fees like implementation and 1-, 2-, or 3-year commitments. This is an indicator of what salespeople are doing as they close deals.

KEEP

This revenue bucket is all about retention — in other words, reducing churn. We defined MRR churn as a unit metric in chapter 4. You can also calculate churn based on users, not just revenue.

Retained MRR is the MRR from the subscribers in the previous month. Start with all of the subscribers who are with you this month. The retained MRR is the MRR those subscribers paid you the last month.

Customer Lifetime is like LTV, except it's measured in years instead of dollars. It's interesting to see how many years an average subscriber subscribes. The trend could be informative. It is good to know if your customers are staying longer or not.

ARPCS means average revenue per churned subscriber. This metric indicates the dollar value to you of subscribers you are losing. You want to watch the trend to see if it's growing or shrinking. You also want to compare this to ARPS to know if you are losing your best subscribers.

Contracted Churn Rate is crucial to watch if you sign long term contracts with your clients. This percentage is calculated by the number of subscribers who churned divided by the number of subscribers who could have churned, meaning they weren't under contract. For example, assume a company has 120 customers, and they are all on an annual contract, evenly spaced so 10 contracts expire each month. If they have two customers unsubscribe in a month, their nominal churn rate is only 2/120, or less than 2%. However, if only 10 of their customers were *eligible* to unsubscribe, their Contracted Churn Rate is 2/10 or 20%. It tells a very different story.

GROW

These metrics watch and describe revenue growth from your current customer base, and they come into play later in the product life cycle. The fastest-growing subscription companies manage these intentionally.

Expansion MRR tracks the third revenue bucket: Grow. To calculate this, start with the total subscribers' revenue this month who were also subscribers last month. Then, subtract the revenue those same subscribers gave you last month. This shows how much additional revenue you earned from your subscriber base. For this metric, ignore churn. Anyone who churned this month doesn't count in the revenue for the previous month.

As an example, assume you have 100 customers. Last month they paid you a total of $10,000. This month there is no churn, and these 100 customers pay you $11,000. Then Expansion MRR is $1,000 ($11,000-$10,000).

In chapter 8, we will break down Expansion MRR into subcategories to help you see where your growth is coming from.

Focusing on GROW revenue should happen *after* you've created an established product and subscriber base. The next chapter will show you why and how this is important, and it will also give you a few additional metrics to track for your expansion efforts.

This may be obvious to you, but remember how we defined three revenue buckets, WIN, KEEP, and GROW? These revenue buckets are the metrics Net New MRR, Retained MRR, and Expansion MRR. Your total MRR for any month is the sum of these three MRRs:

MRR = Net New MRR + Retained MRR + Expansion MRR

In the beginning, a high percentage of your revenue comes from Net New MRR. Then it shifts to Retained

MRR as you build a subscriber base. Eventually, you will focus on Expansion MRR if you want to keep growing.

These metrics are far from exhaustive, but they are the most informative. They point you in the right direction. The key for you is first to determine which revenue bucket you ought to focus on at the moment, then think about and identify which metrics would do a great job of helping you toward success.

Summary

In the early stage of a subscription product, you need to get the product-market fit to have a successful outcome (i.e., a product that sells). Yet, since it's hard to know the value of any individual deal, how can you tell if you've achieved a good fit? This is where the viability metric comes in.

When your viability metric is under three, you should be laser-focused on establishing product-market fit. Narrow your market segment. Improve onboarding and customer retention. You either need to increase LTV or decrease CAC.

After your viability metric exceeds three, ramp up sales and marketing to do more of what you know works.

EXERCISE 5

Determine the viability metric of your current subscription product. Once identified, decide which tactics you should prioritize.

If your viability metric has been over 3 for a while, then create cohorts using market segments and calculate each cohort's viability metric. Are there any cohorts with a viability metric under three?

6

Subscription Growth

———————◆———————

How Fast Should You Grow?

Bessemer Venture Partners has done a great deal of research on privately held subscription companies. One of its metrics is how fast a company grew from $1M to $100M ARR (Annual Recurring Revenue). As of this writing, Slack holds the record: just two years. Twilio took just under five years. Shopify came in at a little over six.

Bessemer categorized these and many more companies into good, better, and best growth rates. (In pricing, we use Good/Better/Best for product packaging, but we'll use Bessemer's meaning for this paragraph.) Their best companies made it from $1M to $100M in under five years, better were under seven, and good were under ten. These same categories showed how quickly these firms grew from $1M to $10M, a more reasonable planning horizon for most companies. Their good, better, and best cutoffs were four, three, and two years, respectively. This means their good companies made it from $1M to $10M in under four years; you may want to remember this particular growth goal since we will use it in chapter 7.

Take a moment to think about your growth goal. How fast do you want your subscription product to go from $1M to $10M or even $100M?

How to Grow Large

There are only two ways to grow your company, win more customers, or increase revenue from your existing customers. WIN and GROW are two of your three revenue buckets. If you want to increase revenue, focus on winning and growing customers. The third bucket, KEEP, is always important, but by definition it doesn't *grow* your company. However, if you don't do a good job of keeping customers, you have to win and grow even more to get ahead.

Think about churn in a growing company. Assume a company has a 2.5% monthly churn, which equates to about 30% annual churn. When the company is only $1M ARR, then they churn $300K per year. The company may win enough new customers to replace this $300K, plus more, to increase revenue. The salesforce just has to work harder. As the company grows to $10M, their churn grows to $3M. At $100M, churn becomes $30M, a *lot* of churn to replace. As a company earns more, it becomes harder to replace lost revenue by winning new customers alone.

As a subscription company grows larger, it needs to shift some energy toward increasing revenue from their current subscribers; in other words, they need to focus on the GROW revenue bucket. If our example company could increase revenue from existing customers by 30%, they would make up for the churn. Then, all new customers become incremental revenue. This is how rapidly-growing subscription companies need to think.

In the early stages of your product's life cycle, you need to focus on winning new customers and learning how to keep them. This doesn't stop in later stages, but if you want to continue to grow rapidly, you need to add attention to increasing revenue from existing customers.

 Impactful Insight

There are only two ways to grow: acquisition and expansion. Over time the importance shifts from winning new customers to growing customers.

NDR — The Ultimate Growth Metric

NDR stands for Net Dollar Retention. For subscription companies in a later growth phase, this is possibly the most critical metric to watch. NDR tells you how fast revenue from existing subscribers is growing or shrinking. Current customers can take one of three actions: buy more, buy the same amount, or buy less (or none). NDR is the aggregation of all of your customers' actions into a single, valuable metric.

Earlier, we discussed churn — existing subscribers choosing not to renew. Churn represents shrinking revenue from your existing customer base and is subtracted from the KEEP bucket. However, some subscribers pay you more based on additional usage or upgrading their choices. Expansion revenue represents how much more these subscribers pay you; it's counted in the GROW bucket. NDR combines the KEEP and GROW buckets while ignoring WIN.

To calculate Net Dollar Retention, start with the MRR you received in an earlier month (a baseline). Subtract lost revenue due to churn, and the result is retained revenue. Add new revenue contributed by expansion. Divide all of that by the original MRR and you have NDR.

NDR = (previous MRR - churn revenue + expansion revenue) / previous MRR

Another way to look at the same formula:

NDR = (retention revenue + expansion revenue) / previous MRR

As a quick reminder, the current period's MRR is the sum of WIN, KEEP, and GROW revenue:

Current period's MRR = acquisition revenue + retention revenue + expansion revenue

Unlike MRR, Net Dollar Retention does not include acquisition revenue (WIN). It only focuses on what is happening with your current subscribers (KEEP and GROW).

Since NDR is usually an annual number, you'll have to convert your monthly numbers into yearly numbers. The easiest way to do this is to use the MRR for December of last year. If nobody churned and nobody bought more, then 12 * December MRR gives you a baseline. Then, by the end of this year, you can see how much revenue you lost from those December subscribers due to churn and how much more some of them bought. To calculate NDR, you don't have to split up retention and expansion, but you will gain more insight if you do.

Notice if revenue churned was precisely equal to expansion revenue, then NDR = 1. This means we get the same revenue all year as we did from the original cohort in December times 12.

Sometimes you may hear the term NDR Growth Rate, which is simply NDR - 1. For example, if there was no churn and expansion revenue was 20% of the baseline, then NDR = 1.2 or 120%. The corresponding NDR Growth Rate is .2 or 20%.

What we're striving for is net dollar retention greater than 100%. Here are some NDR metrics from some successful companies when they filed their S-1 in their initial public offering (IPO).

- Pivotal Software, 158%
- Twilio, 155%
- Atlassian, 148%
- Zoom, 142%
- Elastic NV, 140%
- Pagerduty, 139%
- AppDynamics, 123%
- New Relic, 115%

Take a look at Elastic NV, with 140% NDR. Here's what it means: choose a baseline month (December would be good for a calendar year). Calculate 12*MRR for December to get an annual baseline value. If nobody unsubscribed, then they earned 40% more revenue from those subscribers who were customers in December. However, if they lost a modest 11% of their revenue due to churn, their expansion had to be 100% to make it up. This is due to the way the math works. This should emphasize how critical the GROW revenue is to these companies. In the next chapter, I will explain and give you access to a spreadsheet so you can play with these and figure out your own growth plan.

Impactful Insight

When NDR is over 100%, then all WIN revenue is pure growth.

Summary

As subscription companies grow larger, their focus must include increasing revenue from current subscribers if they want to continue a fast growth rate. The ultimate metric to see this is Net Dollar Retention or NDR. When NDR is over 100%, revenue from current subscribers is growing. Great subscription companies — ones that go public — tend to have NDRs well over 100%.

Zoom example

In the earliest days of Zoom, they were, of course, focused on winning new customers. They needed people using their platform and paying them money. They created loveable products, so users would try them and keep using them.

Zoom has an incredible growth rate. This is because they didn't just focus on winning new customers. They also focused significant energy and effort figuring out how to get their existing customers to buy more. They used strategic pricing metrics, so as a customer grows, they pay more. In Zoom's case, one of their pricing metrics is the number of participants in a session. They use Good/Better/Best packaging to upsell customers to more expensive packages as the customers receive more value.

Using these techniques and others, Zoom has achieved an NDR of 142%. If they had no churn (unlikely), their growth in expansion ARR was 42% per year. Zoom is still doubling in size every year, so we know they also invest heavily in new customer acquisition. But the important takeaway is this: as you grow, focusing on expansion revenue becomes more important.

EXERCISE 6

Calculate your own NDR. Your finance team may already have this number. If not, see if they can give you the data so you can calculate it.

7

Subscription Growth Calculator

———————◆———————

By now, you know subscription companies have three revenue buckets: WIN, KEEP, and GROW. Although each one requires different tactics to improve, you have to manage each bucket separately — this is the challenge. You can't do everything all the time. You have to allocate finite resources across the three buckets.

Additionally, you learned that you should focus on acquisition and retention revenue in the early stages of your subscription business. In the later stages, you should put more focus on expansion revenue. How do you decide what to do when? How do you prioritize?

The Subscription Growth Calculator (SGC) helps you answer these questions. Although the SGC doesn't tell you which resources to invest in each bucket, it does help you plan how much revenue you need each bucket to produce to reach your goals.

Using the Calculator

The SGC tool is built-in Microsoft Excel. Download a copy for your personal use from SGC.impactpricing. com. I have left all of the cells unlocked and visible so you can see every formula and assumption. You can edit them if your situation is different. And, if you completely mess the file up, just download a clean version. However, before changing any formulas, play with it the way it was intended. Only change the cells that are assumptions.

Subscription Growth Calculator

Initial Assumptions

Starting Monthly Revenue	$83,333
Starting # of Subscribers	1,000
# of New Subscribers 1st Month	30

Yearly Assumptions	Sales Growth Rate (monthly)	ARPNS (Monthly)	MRR Churn Rate	Monthly Expansion Rate
Year 1	3.0%	$ 40	-1.0%	6.0%
Year 2	3.0%	$ 40	-1.0%	6.0%
Year 3	3.0%	$ 40	-1.0%	6.0%
Year 4	3.0%	$ 40	-1.0%	6.0%
Year 5	3.0%	$ 40	-1.0%	6.0%

Summary of Results

	Revenue	% of Growth from Acquisition
Year 1	1,497,455	57%
Year 2	2,935,089	48%
Year 3	5,621,559	41%
Year 4	10,595,329	34%
Year 5	19,740,305	28%

	Year 1	Year 2	Year 3	Year 4	Year 5
New Customers					
# New subscribers	426	607	865	1,234	1,759
Sales growth rate	43%	43%	43%	43%	43%
YTD new customers	426	607	865	1,234	1,759
ARPNS	$245.94	$245.94	$245.94	$245.94	$245.94
Acquisition $	$104,712	$149,294	$212,857	$303,483	$432,695
Cohort Existing Jan 1					
Last month's revenue	$142,528	$285,087	$553,505	$1,053,226	$1,975,863
Last month's subscribers	895	1,175	1,585	2,180	3,037
Churn rate	-11%	-11%	-11%	-11%	-11%
Churn $	$ (13,264)	$ (26,531)	$ (51,511)	$ (98,018)	$ (183,882)
Retention $	$ 1,313,158	$ 2,626,607	$ 5,099,634	$ 9,703,740	$ 18,204,318
Expansion rate	101%	101%	101%	101%	101%
Expansion $	$ 79,585	$ 159,188	$ 309,069	$ 588,105	$ 1,103,292
Cohort Revenue	$1,392,743	$2,785,796	$5,408,702	$10,291,845	$19,307,610
NDR rate	139%	139%	139%	139%	139%
Subscribers	886	1,163	1,569	2,158	3,006
ARPS (cohort)	$1,571	$2,395	$3,447	$4,769	$6,422
Totals					
Revenue	$1,497,455	$2,935,089	$5,621,559	$10,595,329	$19,740,305
Subscribers	1,312	1,770	2,434	3,392	4,766
ARPS	$1,141	$1,658	$2,309	$3,124	$4,142
Lifetime	8.8	8.8	8.8	8.8	8.8
LTV	$10,045	$14,594	$20,324	$27,494	$36,457

Subscription Growth Calculator

Step 1 is to set your initial assumptions in these three cells:

Initial Assumptions

Starting Monthly Revenue

$83,333

Starting # of Subscribers

1,000

# of New Subscribers 1st Month

30

Initial Assumptions

You want to put in your real numbers. In our example we chose $83,333 monthly revenue because 12 * $83,333 is $1M in annual revenue. Do you remember the Bessemer Venture numbers in chapter 6? They found "Good" companies went from $1M to $10M in four years. We will see what it takes to make that happen, so we start at $1M. Assume monthly revenue is for December. Starting # of subscribers then is the number of subscribers as of the end of December. The # of new subscribers in the first month is how many new customers you think you will win in January.

Step 2 is to articulate your revenue goal. In this example, we are going to use the goal of $10M in four years.

There is no place on the spreadsheet to enter it, but you can play with the yearly assumptions to see how you might hit your goal. In the figure below, you can see revenue for Year four is $10,595. If you said you wanted $30M in five years, you would look at the revenue for year five, see it is well below the goal and would need to adjust some assumptions to get the number toward your goal.

Summary of Results

	Revenue	% of Growth from Acquisition
Year 1	1,497,455	57%
Year 2	2,935,089	48%
Year 3	5,621,559	41%
Year 4	10,595,329	34%
Year 5	19,740,305	28%

Articulate Revenue Goal

Step 3 is to tweak your yearly assumptions until the revenue shows your goal. These are the yearly assumptions:

Yearly Assumptions	Sales Growth Rate (monthly)	ARPNS (Monthly)	MRR Churn Rate	Monthly Expansion Rate
Year 1	3.0%	$ 40	-1.0%	6.0%
Year 2	3.0%	$ 40	-1.0%	6.0%
Year 3	3.0%	$ 40	-1.0%	6.0%
Year 4	3.0%	$ 40	-1.0%	6.0%
Year 5	3.0%	$ 40	-1.0%	6.0%

Tweak the Yearly Assumptions

All of the numbers here represent monthly data, but they are called yearly assumptions because the number can't change in the middle of the year (for the simplicity of the spreadsheet). Here is what this means:

- We will win 3% more new customers each month than we did the month before
- Each new customer will pay us an average of $40
- Our churn rate is 1% per month
- For a cohort of subscribers, each month, they will pay us 6% more (due to price increases, usage, up-sell, and cross-sell).

At first, only change the cells in yellow. This will also change all the cells below them. However, if you want to see what happens if you shifted more resources into expansion over time, you could enter values anywhere on this table.

Step 4 is to interpret the results. We now look at the resulting numbers and ask if this is feasible. Can we win 3% more customers each month? We might have to invest more in sales and marketing to make it happen. Can we achieve $40 ARPNS? Maybe we need to change pricing or the product packaging. Is -1% churn rate reasonable, or do we need to invest more in onboarding and customer success? Can we get customers to pay us 6% more on average each month? Maybe we need to rethink our pricing metrics, our upsell packaging or create some cross-sell products. These yearly assumption numbers are what you need to hit to reach your overall goal.

Summary of Results

	Revenue	% of Growth from Acquisition
Year 1	1,497,455	57%
Year 2	2,935,089	48%
Year 3	5,621,559	41%
Year 4	10,595,329	34%
Year 5	19,740,305	28%

Summary of Results

Let's look at the summary of the results once again. Notice the amount of growth coming from acquisition decreases as a percentage of your business. This is an indicator of acquisition becoming less critical as you grow.

What if you have a set of yearly assumptions that gives you the growth results you want, but you don't believe you can meet those objectives? Keep playing. Just for fun, I created another set of yearly assumptions that also got us to $10M by year four. Notice we started with a heavy emphasis on acquisition growth and little focus on expansion. Over the years, those two positions switched.

Yearly Assumptions	Sales Growth Rate (monthly)	ARPNS (Monthly)	MRR Churn Rate	Monthly Expansion Rate
Year 1	7.0%	$ 40	-1.0%	3.0%
Year 2	6.0%	$ 50	-1.0%	4.0%
Year 3	5.0%	$ 60	-1.0%	5.0%
Year 4	4.0%	$ 70	-1.0%	6.0%
Year 5	3.0%	$ 80	-1.0%	6.0%

Alternate Assumptions

Which set of yearly assumptions do you think are more achievable for your product or company? This is the spreadsheet's whole point — to figure out how you will reach your overall revenue goal.

Yearly Assumptions	Sales Growth Rate (monthly)	ARPNS (Monthly)	MRR Churn Rate	Monthly Expansion Rate
Year 1	10.5%	$ 40	-1.0%	0.0%
Year 2	10.5%	$ 40	-1.0%	0.0%
Year 3	10.5%	$ 40	-1.0%	0.0%
Year 4	10.5%	$ 40	-1.0%	0.0%
Year 5	10.5%	$ 40	-1.0%	0.0%

Summary of Results

	Revenue	% of Growth from Acquisition
Year 1	1,078,483	100%
Year 2	1,596,086	100%
Year 3	3,536,130	100%
Year 4	10,164,551	100%
Year 5	32,307,440	100%

Assume No Expansion Revenue

Here is one more example with a fascinating insight. I set the monthly expansion rate to 0%, meaning there is no expansion revenue (the GROW bucket). We set a modest churn rate of -1% per month. Then, we played with the sales growth rate to get to $10M in revenue in year 4. This requires 10.5% per month growth, which works out to 231% growth per year. This means you have to more than triple your new customer acquisition every year to reach your goal — a very challenging target. Here is one conclusion I hope you take away from this: to have a fast growth rate, you MUST create pricing and packaging that encourages customers to buy more from you.

Metrics

Earlier in the book, we described various metrics. You see many of them in the section on the right side of the SGC.

	Year 1	Year 2
New Customers		
# New subscribers	661	2,191
Sales growth rate	231%	231%
YTD new customers	**661**	**2,191**
ARPNS	$213.52	$213.52
Acquisition $	**$141,162**	**$467,805**
Cohort Existing Jan 1		
Last month's revenue	$74,611	$89,812
Last month's subscribers	895	1,386
Churn rate	-11%	-11%
Churn $	$ (9,468)	$ (11,397)
Retention $	$ 937,321	$ 1,128,281
Expansion rate	0%	0%
Expansion $	$ -	$ -
Cohort Revenue	**$937,321**	**$1,128,281**
NDR rate	**94%**	**94%**
Subscribers	886	1,372
ARPS (cohort)	$1,057	$823
Totals		
Revenue	**$1,078,483**	**$1,596,086**
Subscribers	1,548	3,563
ARPS	$697	$448
Lifetime	8.8	8.8
LTV	$6,134	$3,943

Unit Metrics

Of particular interest are the three revenue buckets. They are calculated and labeled: acquisition, retention, and expansion. These three revenue buckets are what you are measuring and managing; the sum of them makes up your overall revenue.

The SGC does have limitations: for example, anyone who subscribes during the year is counted as acquisition revenue for the remainder of that year. We also assume none of them churn out or buy more during the year they initially subscribe. The following year, they become part of the cohort we use to estimate retention and expansion revenue.

Let's take a closer look at Net Dollar Retention. As you can see in the metrics displayed above, the initial assumptions resulted in a calculated 139% NDR. That is pretty close to Zoom's NDR of 142%. Here's a hint as you play with the spreadsheet: to achieve this NDR, your MRR churn rate and your monthly expansion rate need to total 5%. For example, 6% + -1% = 5%. If your churn were 0%, an expansion rate of 5% would give you the same results.

Impactful Insight

Use the subscription growth calculator to determine how much of your revenue needs to come from the WIN, KEEP, and GROW revenue buckets to hit your overall growth goals. This should guide your resource allocation and your effort.

I hope it's evident by this point that achieving rapid growth requires ample execution and attention on all three revenue buckets. Acquisition and retention (WIN and KEEP, respectively) have always been obvious to subscription companies. They are rarely ignored. Yet far too many companies ignore expansion (GROW). The rest of this section dives into how you ought to think about expansion.

Summary

The Subscription Growth Calculator (SGC) was created to help you achieve your growth goals by identifying and prioritizing which revenue buckets you should focus on at any given time.

EXERCISE 7

What revenue do you expect to have in four or five years? Write it down. Play with the SGC to figure out how fast you need to grow your WIN, KEEP, and GROW revenue buckets to achieve your goal. Find several combinations you could implement to hit your goal. Which seems most feasible?

8

Implementing expansion

———————◆———————

You now know expansion revenue is crucial to rapid growth, but you may be wondering how to do it. After all, this isn't something traditional businesses typically focus on. Before thinking about how to implement expansion for your market, think about how to grow revenue from a single customer.

There are four ways to grow revenue from a customer:
1. Usage
2. Upsell
3. Price increases
4. Cross-sell

These are also closely related to the three value levers we saw earlier: market segmentation, packaging, and pricing metrics. Let's go through each one.

Usage

Two factors can cause increased usage of your product. First, as users learn more about your subscription, its capabilities, and how much value it really can deliver, they may use it more often.

When I first started using Hubspot CRM to help with sales, I used very few of its capabilities. I could add a contact, some notes, send an email, and complete a follow-up task. As I used it more, I learned about templates, sequences, managing deals, and sending videos as emails. There is probably still a ton I don't know how to use. The point is, as I learn more about what it can do and how to do it, I use Hubspot even more. I'll tie this specifically to pricing in a moment.

The second reason subscribers use more is their needs may increase. Imagine a company subscribed when they had revenue of $1M, and now they have grown to $5M. They have more customers, more employees, more transactions, more data, and more assets. Since they have grown, they may need to use the subscription product more.

In both of these cases, as subscribers use more of your product, they receive more value. As usage increases, what we need is a pricing metric to capture some of their increased value.

Remember, a pricing metric is what you charge for. If you charge by the employee, then as a company grows and hires more employees, they pay you more. If you charge by the GB of storage, then a company or user with increasing amounts of data will pay you more. There are many possible pricing metrics you could use.

We won't go into the details of how to choose a pricing metric here, but as a quick reminder, you want your pricing metric to be correlated with your customer's value metric. A value metric is how your customer measures your value to them. Customers may have many different value metrics, and you will want to brainstorm as many as possible.

To get you started, imagine your customer saying this sentence — a value metric fills in the blanks: "I love your company because our _____ went from _____ to _____." For example, "I love Salesforce because our revenue per salesperson went from $3M to $3.5M." Or, "I love our new pricing system because our quote time went from two weeks to two hours."

Once you have a useful pricing metric, your Customer Success department should help users get more value out of your product, so they use it more. The more they use, the more they pay.

Upsell

As buyers learn more about your subscription and its capabilities, and as they become more familiar with your user interfaces, they struggle less and realize how beneficial your product is. With less time spent learning, they look to see what other value you might be able to add. This is typically when they upgrade to a new package. They pay you more because they want to be able to do more, because of the greater value you're giving them.

Upgrading also happens as companies grow. Larger companies tend to have different needs than smaller companies. Large companies likely need better security, better collaboration tools, and better reporting capabilities. Imagine if security, collaboration, and reporting were not included in the base product. As the company grows, they may choose to buy some of those additional capabilities from you, and therefore pay you more.

Upsell is entirely dependent on your packaging. Think of this as the process by which features are bundled together or priced separately. The most powerful packaging technique for most companies is Good/Better/Best, plus options. This allows customers to try out your product at relatively low risk with the Good package. As they learn more and want more, they may upgrade to Better or Best or choose to purchase an option. In each case, they pay you more.

One of the hardest decisions to make for a subscription is which features should go in which package and which features should be offered as options. As some quick guidance, your Good product should be like a minimum viable product. It provides the minimum functionality a user needs to get real value out of your product (without falling significantly short of what competitors offer for a comparable price).

Better is probably what most of your users would want. Best applies to a small portion of your users. They are the ones with a high willingness to pay for features only they really value and would pay dearly for. Last, options should include the features wanted by less than 50% of buyers who are *not* all buyers of the best product. Options should also be somewhat expensive because you don't want to manage a ton of inexpensive options, *and* your buyers don't want to be "nickeled and dimed" to death.

After you have created a compelling portfolio, your customer success department has an important role to play once again. Helping a customer be as successful as possible with whatever package they purchased increases the likelihood the customer will upgrade.

Raise Prices

Don't you hate it when a subscription service that you depend on raises their prices? But what do you do? You keep paying it. Nobody likes price increases, but they happen. Subscription companies have some key advantages when it comes to raising prices.

One key advantage is the increasing value a subscriber receives over time. This value grows for several reasons. First, as users become more familiar with the product, they can make it do more to get more value. Next, the subscription vendor has likely added more capability over time, fixing bugs, tweaking UI's, and adding new significant features. All of these add more value than when the user first subscribed. Finally, switching costs for the user have probably grown over time as well. Subscribers design their workflow around this subscription product. Sometimes, they may have created a large amount of content that would be costly to port to another system (consider Atlassian's JIRA or Confluence). Changing vendors requires a large investment in new learning and workflow, and sometimes redesign and porting costs.

For these reasons, although subscribers may not like price increases, they tend to accept them. They realize paying a small amount more is a lot better than shopping for an alternative and then enduring the significant effort required to change their processes to adopt it.

Raising prices becomes so much easier and more effective when you clearly understand your market segments (the remaining value lever). Knowing your market segment lets you deliver even more value to that segment, giving you room to raise prices. This may be a great time to split the product up into variants for different market segments so that you can charge different prices for those different segments. The ones who have always received way more value than they paid for can now start paying more. Yes, they will complain, but they will pay it if they are genuinely receiving the value.

If you choose to raise prices, there are several considerations: Who, How, and Why. Let's start with Who. It's hard to raise prices on existing customers without also raising prices on new customers. This is especially true for any prices displayed on your website. Plan on raising prices for new buyers first. However, remember that over time, you've added more capability to your product. More people are using it, and you likely also have more positive word of mouth, so your reputation is probably better than it used to be. Buyers perceive less of a risk now. If you've truly been successful with your current subscribers, raising prices may not be that much of a threat to new business.

Also, consider markets that are becoming saturated. If there are not many new customers to win, the raising prices on new customers isn't painful. For example, most companies in the SMB (Small-Medium Business) segment are already using some financial management software. When Intuit raised my rates on QuickBooks Online, of course, I grumbled and then paid it. Yet, even if having higher rates for new customers slowed their customer acquisition pace, the additional money they made from companies like mine by raising prices would have more than made up for it.

One more insight into the Who: if you only raise prices on new customers, they don't even know you raised prices because they weren't paying the lower price in the first place. Of course, you miss out on the increased revenue you could have received from your current customers.

The second consideration is How. My recommendation for raising prices on existing customers is to roll them out in a phased manner. It's true: people hate price increases. When you raise the price on a subscriber, they will be prompted to rethink their decision. Before you raised the price, the subscriber probably paid you automatically — rarely, if ever, thinking about their choice to remain a subscriber. After all, they already thought hard about this choice, finally decided, and then implemented it. They don't want to rethink the decision every month. However, once you raise the price, they will think, "is this subscription really worth it?"

Hence, you want to minimize the number of people who choose to churn when they rethink the decision. The way to do this is by using a phased price increase. Start by only increasing the prices on the customers who get the most value from your product. Which ones are those? Probably the ones who use your product the most. Customer usage is a reasonable proxy for value and willingness to pay.

Create an overall measure of usage and then sort customers from the highest usage to the lowest. Next, raise prices on the top 20% heaviest users. Monitor what happens. How many churned? Did you make more money on the price increase than you lost due to churn? If so, raise prices on the next 20%. Again, what happened? If the second price increase was profitable, raise prices on the third 20%. What happened? Probably in the third or fourth batch of price increases, you will either be upside down or close to break-even on whether or not it was profitable. Once you find that point, don't raise prices on those with lower usage.

You probably will never raise prices on the bottom 20% of users. Here's why: these are the people who are paying your bill month after month without thinking about it, but they probably aren't getting enough value. When you raise their price, they'll rethink their decision, and they will likely churn. Many of us have purchased an expensive gym membership only to rarely use it (if ever). And yet, we kept paying the bill. What would have happened if you received a notice that the gym price went up by 10%? Many people would think, "I'm not even using it. I should get rid of it." In other words, let sleeping dogs lie.

A key consideration when it comes to raising prices is to do something nice for your customers. Netflix has executed both horrible and terrific price increases. You probably recall in 2011 when they dramatically raised prices on all of their subscribers and subsequently lost 800,000 subscribers (including me).

Several years later, they tried again — and this time, they saw much better results. They sent their subscribers an email saying they'd increased prices, but since you're a good customer, they will hold your price at the current level for a year. Eleven months later, you got another email reminding you they raised prices a year ago, and now it's time for you to pay more. This price increase went over much better. Consider doing something nice for your existing customers to make them feel special as you raise their price.

The third and final consideration is Why. Your market needs a reason. They will hate you if they think you are just raising prices to make more profit, so give them a reason.

When their prices are being increased, the single best reason customers accept is rising costs. If you've ever been in one of my pricing classes, you know I've pounded into you that costs don't matter to pricing. And they don't (almost never). But, your buyers don't know this. When we explain to customers that our costs went up or are going up, they are much more likely to accept the price increase.

One of my favorite price increase letters recently came from Netflix. They said they have to raise our prices so they can continue to invest in original content. Sounds great, but it's just not true. Fixed costs have absolutely *nothing* to do with pricing. Never, never, never!

Price increases in subscriptions are a powerful way to grow revenue from individual customers. However, be sure to do it wisely.

Cross-sell

Cross-sell is the last of the techniques to grow existing customer revenue. Before implementing this, your subscription product should be well established, you will have built a great brand, and your customers should love you. Now, what other products could you develop and sell to help those same customers? Because they know and love you in one area, they are more likely to trust you in another area.

Suppose you accept Pragmatic Institute's definition of a market segment as a set of buyers and users with common problems. In that case, you could think of cross-selling as creating new products to target different market segments within your current customers.

As an example, I use Hubspot Sales CRM tools to help with my business. I do not use their Marketing CRM tools. One day I might decide to purchase their Marketing tools for my marketing team, but they solve a different set of problems. Their marketing tools are a cross-sell item to those of us who are only using Sales CRM.

Other companies use Hubspot's Marketing CRM Tools without using their sales tools. To those companies, Sales CRM is a possible cross-sell item. The Sales CRM and Marketing Tools are stand-alone products, but they work well together.

The defining line between upsell and cross-sell is often gray, but it doesn't matter. When you get to this stage, you should be thinking about what else you could provide your customers that may not be directly related to your current product.

Impactful Insight

There are four ways to grow a customer, and none of them happen by accident. Expansion must be planned.

Market Segments

As we saw earlier, market segments are incredibly valuable when deciding to raise prices, but they are equally useful in the other three techniques for growing customer revenue.

Companies with clearly defined market segments choose effective pricing metrics to capture more value as subscribers increase their usage. When market segments are well defined, companies can successfully create different pricing metrics for each market segment.

The same is true with packaging. Different market segments value different features differently. To take full advantage of this, you would create different Good/Better/

Best packages for each market segment. Your upsell efforts will be much more effective when your packages are designed for specific market segments.

Cross-sell is possibly the most interesting because you may be able to use the products and packages you created for different market segments as cross-sells.

LinkedIn is an incredible example for all of these. LinkedIn has defined four market segments: salespeople, recruiters, job seekers, and professionals. The last segment is a catch-all for business people who want to connect with other business people. Within each of these market segments, LinkedIn has created different price levels, different product packaging, and different pricing metrics. They can also increase the revenue from their existing subscribers by using all of the techniques in this chapter, targeted at their specific market segments.

Here is my favorite aspect of LinkedIn's implementation: although it is quite complicated, with all of these market segments and permutations, it looks simple from the buyer's perspective. Once a buyer identifies their market segment, the products and prices offered to them are logical and straightforward.

Summary

Traditional companies rarely focus on expansion revenue, but if subscription companies want to continue growing after they become large, they must. You may have heard the phrase "land and expand". The expand part is all about the GROW revenue bucket. And it doesn't happen by accident — you need to plan for it and then take action to make it happen.

There are four ways to get more revenue from a customer: usage, upsell, price increase, and cross-sell. However, to do these effectively, you need to master the three value levers discussed in chapter 3.

EXERCISE 8

What strategies or tactics could you use to increase revenue
in the GROW bucket?

- How can you increase usage? Do you have the right pricing metrics?
- How can you convince customers to upgrade? Do you have the right packaging?
- How can you implement a price increase? Have you targeted market segments?
- How can you get them to buy other products from you? Do you have additional offerings?

9

Prioritizing Expansion

———————◆———————

By now, you realize expansion revenue is crucial to growing your business in the long run. Here's the problem: it isn't urgent. You must force it to be a priority to benefit from its power.

Why Expansion is Ignored

As represented in the figure below, when a company first releases a subscription, acquisition revenue is most important; they must quickly win new customers. As soon as the company starts winning customers, they quickly realize how equally important retention is. Hence, both acquisition revenue and retention revenue are in the upper right of the graph. In the early days of a subscription, expansion revenue is entirely irrelevant. It is neither urgent nor important.

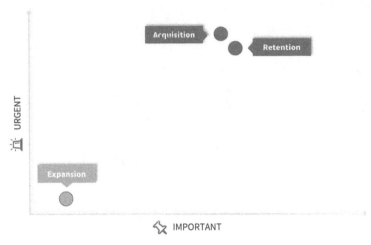

Why Expansion Is Ignored In Early Stages

As a subscription business grows, winning new customers becomes much less important and also less urgent. We saw this when we looked at the subscription growth calculator. Retention may get a little less attention, but it generates most of the revenue, so companies watch it very closely. We also saw in the subscription growth calculator how expansion revenue becomes more important to growing companies. But does it ever become urgent?

Think about urgency by considering negative consequences. In the early days, both acquisition and retention revenues determine company survival. If you don't figure them out quickly, the company fails. Hence, they are both urgent.

Now think about urgency at a later stage. If churn isn't under control, the company struggles a lot, so negative changes in churn remain urgent to solve. Now let's assume the company has churn under control. Even if they don't win a ton of new customers, they don't suffer because they have a large subscriber base paying them. The growth rate is slower, but that's like getting a bowl of ice cream for dessert, not knowing you could have had a bigger bowl. New customer acquisition is much less urgent. The same is true for expansion. A company that doesn't focus on expansion doesn't even realize they can grow faster. In this situation, they feel no pain in ignorance. There is no urgency in expansion.

Remember, expansion is important. It is the primary driver of growth for later-stage subscriptions. As you can see in the figure below, expansion becomes important over time but never becomes urgent.

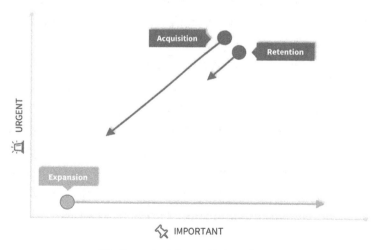

Why Expansion Is Ignored In Later Stages

Creating Urgency

Assuming you're convinced of the importance of expansion revenue, now you have to make it urgent and motivate people in your company to focus on it. You can do this with metrics. Measuring and publishing metrics inside a company tends to make the driver of the metric more urgent. After all, "what gets measured gets managed" — this is what you want to create.

It's unlikely the entire company will suddenly grow a sense of urgency about expansion revenue, but individual employees will. As an example, their negative consequences could be embarrassment or not getting a promotion.

Once you decide expansion revenue is important, start by calculating net dollar retention and expansion MRR as the overall metrics. Then, you want to manage and improve these results using more granular metrics described in the next few paragraphs.

Every subscriber who paid you more this month than last month did so for one of four reasons: they used more, they upgraded, you raised prices, or they bought something new. It could also be a combination of these reasons. You want to allocate the increase in revenue from each subscriber to one or more of these four reasons. To be fair, if you had subscribers who paid you less but did not churn out, you should also allocate their decrease in revenue to these reasons.

The four reasons a customer would pay you more can be measured and are metrics you want to watch regularly: New Usage MRR, Upsell MRR, Price Increase MRR, and Cross-sell MRR. The sum of these four new KPIs will equal the expansion MRR.

These metrics also represent the four subscriber behaviors your marketing and salespeople can influence. Just like each marketing and sales tactic targets one of the three revenue buckets (WIN, KEEP, and GROW), when you focus on growing revenue, then each tactic also needs to be aimed at modifying one of these subscriber behaviors.

As mentioned in chapter 8, expansion doesn't happen by accident. You have to take action to make it happen. Setting your goals and watching each of these metrics' trends shows which tactics are working for you and clarifies your future emphasis. You may even assign the responsibility of managing these more detailed metrics to specific individuals. Metric trend lines work magic at creating urgency.

Impactful Insight

Expansion is only urgent when you make it urgent. Monitoring the right KPI's can make it urgent.

Summary

The GROW revenue bucket is often overlooked or given minimal attention and resources because it never becomes explicitly urgent. If you want to grow your subscription as rapidly as possible, you need to make expansion urgent and manage it.

The easiest way to do both is to use four new metrics measuring the four ways you can grow a customer: usage, upsell, higher prices, and cross-sell. When responsibility for increasing one of these is assigned to an individual, the metric becomes urgent.

EXERCISE 9

Calculate these four metrics for your own subscription product over time.

- New Usage MRR
- Upsell MRR
- Price Increase MRR
- Cross-sell MRR

    Are they trending the way you think they should?

Section 3.

Transitioning to Subscriptions

If your company has been in business for any length of time, you probably started selling products one or more at a time. We call this a traditional business, one that isn't based on subscriptions. If this describes you and you've gotten this far in the book it must be because you want to shift toward subscriptions. You now know all of the benefits, and you want some of them for your company.

However, as a traditional business, you must overcome some significant hurdles — hurdles companies "born in the cloud" don't face. You have already built a business, created a culture, and implemented systems to make your processes more efficient and effective. You don't get to start over. You need to convince almost every department and every employee to think and behave differently. This is not an easy task.

What follows in the upcoming chapters are many issues you face that your newer competitors don't.

Even though you face challenges they don't, you also have a big head start understanding your markets and their problems. You have built a brand and reputation in the market. If you believe your market will eventually go to subscriptions, then you need to get there first. Start being aggressive. Pursue this with commitment — because if you don't, someone else will.

10

Why Make the Move to Subscription?

———◆———

First, and most importantly, why are you going to a subscription model? There are many great reasons why this may be good for your business, but those don't matter right now. You must specifically think about whether your *customers* would prefer to buy a subscription over owning your product. Companies make money by solving problems for their customers. How does a subscription help your customers solve their problems better than a traditional business?

There are many possible reasons your customers prefer a subscription, but you need them to be compelling. If you usually lock customers into a 3-year contract, you may be thinking of just dividing your product's price by 36 months and charging them the resulting figure each month. Some will stay beyond their contract, so we make more money, and our investors are happy we're selling subscriptions. It seems win-win.

This is *horrible* thinking. A subscription is not a payment plan. It's a business model. Technically, you do have a subscription, but you've missed out on the value and power of subscriptions. You aren't taking advantage of all of the concepts discussed in earlier chapters: you haven't designed an upsell or cross-sell with your packaging, you haven't thoughtfully chosen a pricing metric, and so on. You are thinking about yourself and not about your customers.

Impactful Insight
A subscription is not a payment plan. It's a business model.

Think deeply about the benefits your buyers are trying to achieve by buying your product. Think also about any negative aspects of buying your product. Then, if you could re-create a set of products and services to help a buyer get those benefits *and more* each month while reducing the negative aspects, you've created a potentially powerful subscription. If you don't think this way, a competitor will come along and disrupt your industry by doing precisely this.

Let's think through a fun example. Porsche created an attractive business model where you can subscribe to a Porsche. First question: what are the benefits people want when they buy a Porsche? To drive it, obviously. Their self-perception when they are seen driving it. For the fun of driving a sports car: fast cornering, incredible acceleration. To have a sexy SUV (Cayenne) instead of a minivan. There are many more.

Second question: what are the negative aspects of buying a Porsche? Huge upfront investment. Insurance is high. A family doesn't fit in a 2-seater. Routine maintenance is expensive. There are, of course, more.

Final question: can you deliver those benefits *plus more* every month while eliminating some negative aspects? The Porsche subscription is $2,000 or $3,000 per month (depending on which types of cars you want to choose from). You can drive any vehicle you wish to in your selected category. You can also take it back to the dealership and trade for another car any time you want. They cover maintenance and insurance, and you are only responsible for the gas.

Now, go back through the answers to the first two questions. Notice this subscription offering still gives all of the benefits of owning a Porsche. It eliminates all of the negative aspects we listed, too — although subscriptions won't always work that way. And, the subscription gives even more benefits that weren't even considered before. There is a lower risk because someone can subscribe for a relatively low monthly payment to try it and then unsubscribe if they don't like it. A subscriber can drive a different Porsche each week, which isn't feasible when owning the car.

Porsche still sells many cars, so not every customer is jumping on the subscription bandwagon with them. However, many are. Porsche subscriptions are expanding into more cities. They have found an effective product formula for a market segment. It doesn't have to work for everyone, but it should work for a large enough segment to make it worthwhile. It's possible Porsche is attracting a new market segment: buyers who wouldn't buy a Porsche but are happy to subscribe to one.

The point is to create a subscription product, not a payment plan. Your transition is a chance to build a great solution to solve even more problems than you do with your traditional products. When you do this, you have a much better chance of achieving your internal objectives for going to subscriptions.

Impactful Insight

Your new subscription product must be better than your traditional product for your buyers.

Summary

You probably want to transition to a subscription for all of the benefits your company could receive, but that's not enough. You must think through it from your customer's perspective. Will they get the same benefits? But more importantly, will they receive additional benefits?

Cloud vs Subscription

In the software world, these two terms are used almost interchangeably, but they shouldn't be. They have two very different meanings.

Cloud is a software implementation where the smarts and data are on a cloud-based server typically controlled by the supplier. The opposite of this was on-premise software where the smarts and data were on servers

Can you also overcome some of the negatives of owning your current products (instead of subscribing to them)? This is what makes it reasonable — and powerful — to shift to subscriptions.

owned and maintained by the users, usually at their site.

Subscription is a periodic payment for a regular delivery of benefits. In software, the opposite of this was a perpetual license where the buyer owns the software.

They are commonly used interchangeably because companies who previously sold perpetually licensed on-premise software moved to cloud implementations. They often switched to subscription business models at the same time. Though most cloud software is now subscription-based and most subscription software is cloud-based, the terms are not interchangeable.

EXERCISE 10

From your customer's perspective, what are the benefits and challenges of buying your traditional product? For your new subscription product, can you deliver all of the benefits – plus more – while eliminating some of the challenges?

11
Cultural Shift

———————◆———————

Let's assume you have created an excellent subscription product, and it gives customers many more benefits than your traditional product. This is a great start, but you still have some pretty big cultural challenges ahead of you.

Usage matters

Here comes an aha moment. When you sell a perpetual license or a product, you don't really care if your customer uses it (unless you need the customer to serve as a reference for other prospective customers). You might talk about caring, but you don't — not really. You already received your money; you were paid for the product, not for the benefits it can deliver.

In subscriptions, customers are buying the *benefits* (not the product) with periodic payments. If you fail to deliver those benefits regularly, they will stop paying you — so you *have* to care if they are using your product *and* if they are using it correctly.

Your company mindset has to shift away from selling products toward getting customers to use and love your products!

Subscription companies have a department you may not have heard of before called Customer Success. You may have had a Customer Service or Customer Support department whose job is to answer customer questions. These are *reactive*. Your Customer Success department must be *proactive*.

Customer Success activities typically start with onboarding: when a new customer subscribes, you help them learn to use your product quickly — this ensures they begin receiving the benefits they wanted quickly, too.

The time it takes a new customer to get value from your product is called time to value. The faster you get someone to receive benefits, the less likely they are to churn out quickly.

Once customers are up and running, your Customer Success team is "watching" their usage to see if they continue to receive value. Maybe they can find ways to increase the amount of value your customer receives. These are often done through algorithms watching customer activity. When your customers receive more value, you see a great result: customers don't churn out. They're more likely to increase their use of your product, which means you make more money if you have the right pricing metric.

They are more likely to upgrade to a better package, more likely to trust you enough to buy other products from you, and they are more likely to accept a price increase.

As you can see, usage truly matters when running a subscription business: this is a significant shift compared to a traditional business.

Impactful Insight

Ensuring customers USE your product is much more important in a subscription business.

Three Revenue Buckets

When running your traditional business, you probably focused a lot on sales. Your marketing team finds new leads and passes them off to sales for the close. Almost all of the revenue comes from winning new deals this way.

In the subscription world, however, this changes. You now have three revenue buckets you need to watch and manage: WIN, KEEP, and GROW.

WIN

This is what your business focused on since inception — nothing much changes here. Marketing finds leads. Sales closes deals. What does change, though, is how you structure the deal, how you compensate your sales team, and how you recognize revenue. We will talk about these later in this chapter.

KEEP

This is something traditional companies didn't have to think about before. Customers paid you, and you delivered the product; the transaction was done. With subscriptions, you need customers to pay you month after month, year after year. All of a sudden, churn is essential. You begin to wonder why people leave. One way to prevent churn is through your Customer Success team. They may be able to identify the characteristics of subscribers who are about to leave, so you can try to do something to stop them from churning.

Churn will generally not be a problem if you have a great product, you sell only to customers who value your benefits, and you make sure they receive the benefits they expect (and more). When too many customers are unsubscribing, it's likely because you're failing in one of these three areas.

GROW

Traditional companies spend some energy and time thinking about earning more revenue from customers, such as cross-selling. After all, if someone bought one product from us, might they buy something else? However, as mentioned previously, traditional companies prioritize winning customers, not keeping or growing them. The focus must be different in a subscription business when it comes to earning revenue.

In previous chapters, we discussed some of the ways to earn more revenue from your customers. Here's a quick reminder:

First, you now need to decide on your pricing metric. What are you going to charge for? When you do this well, customers pay you more money as they use more of your product.

Second, you want to think a little differently about your packaging. You're now thinking about how to package your features so the people who get the most value from your product upgrade to higher packages or buy more options.

Deal structure

Monthly or contracts

Traditional businesses switching to subscriptions tend not to trust future revenue will come. They try to get their customers to sign a 3-year contract. After all, when their sales team closed a deal under a traditional model, they usually earned about that much. However, this is detrimental thinking.

If you *can* close deals like the 3-year contract example, more power to you — but you give up some of the power of a subscription. Buyers like subscriptions in part because they can buy in at a lower price, and they know they can leave if it doesn't work out as expected. They have much lower risk, meaning you make a sale more easily.

If you have a great product, deliver real value, only sell to the right customers, *and* **make sure** they are getting the value from your product, they will not only subscribe but stay! Do you have faith in your product, Sales team, and Customer Success department?

The subscription business is about building a trusting relationship and delivering value consistently to your subscribers. Contracts are about locking in customers so they can't leave if you fail to deliver on your promises.

My consistent recommendation on the deal structure is to offer a monthly price. This is for several reasons: it lowers the risk for someone to get into your product; it demonstrates that you believe in your product; and it makes it easier to win deals, meaning it lowers your Customer Acquisition Cost (CAC). You can also offer an annual (or longer) subscription at a reduced price. Buyers can self-select the more extended agreement if they aren't risk-averse or already know your product well.

If you aren't offering a monthly price, is it because you aren't confident you can keep subscribers from churning? If that's the case, should you be offering a subscription?

Upfront Implementation Costs

Sometimes there is a significant cost to onboarding a new customer. There could be a hardware component or a large installation, configuration, or data migration effort. It is understandable companies wouldn't want to implement all of this without some commitment in return. Here are three ways to handle this and some of their pros and cons.

Implementation fee: You could charge a fee to cover your costs. This takes the risk of a loss away from you, but it also makes it harder for Sales to close a deal. If you go down this path, don't think of professional services as a profit center. Cover your costs, but don't make the job ridiculously hard for Sales. Use the subscription to make a profit, not the implementation fees.

In this circumstance, you have another advantage: when a buyer commits to an upfront fee, they are much less likely to churn. They demonstrated commitment, and they realize if they switch, they will likely have to pay a similar fee to the next supplier as well.

Contract: You could choose the annual (or longer) contract and amortize your implementation costs across the monthly payments. This still moves the risk to the customer and makes it harder for salespeople to close deals, but it's less abrasive to the customer than having an upfront fee.

Trust your process: You could just increase the subscription price to make sure the costs are covered in a reasonable time, without requiring a contract. In this case, you are taking the risk. If you have the right product and the right customer, they will stay. Do this well, and the lifetime value of your customer is even larger. Your customers won't even know you indirectly charged an implementation fee.

Sales Compensation

If you have a direct sales force, sales compensation will become a big issue when shifting to subscriptions. Let's examine the problem.

Let's say your traditional product sold for $360,000, and your sales commission rate is 5%, so a salesperson makes $18,000 every time they sell a product.

You move to a subscription model, and it's pretty common to charge the customer about 1/36th of the regular price as the monthly subscription price, which assumes a 3-year break-even. Now a salesperson closes a deal for $1,000 the first month. If they still get a 5% commission, they now only receive $50. This is not going to motivate a salesperson.

You have to solve this problem if you expect salespeople to perform. Compensation drives sales behavior, so it can't be an afterthought. There isn't a single best answer — but here are some ideas for you to consider when deciding what will work best for your company.

Pay based on contract value

If you didn't heed my earlier advice and instead direct your salespeople to sell 3-year contracts, you *could* choose to compensate them based on the contract value. This is the most manageable sales commission plan, but as discussed above, you lose a big part of the value of the subscription model.

Pay based on recurring revenue

Your company is willing to take revenue over time, so your salespeople may be as well. This is a low financial risk for your company, but your salespeople bear the risk. They may not accept this happily and may decide to leave your company. If this happens, you could end up with a more significant — and more expensive — problem: having to re-staff your sales team.

If you can create and implement a compensation model based on recurring revenue without losing your salespeople, you may want to consider imposing a limit. Take the 3-year contract example above: three years after closing the sale, the salesperson should have matched or exceeded their previous commission. Beyond those three years, they continue earning a commission, so in 3 to 5 years, they could be making the same annual commission but not selling anything new. To keep them motivated to sell consistently, you may opt to pay commissions for only the first three years of a new customer's subscription.

Pay based on the expected lifetime

You can estimate or calculate an expected customer lifetime. Let's say it's 24 months. You could pay salespeople the commission upfront, assuming the customer will stay for 24 months. Salespeople like this, of course, because they receive their commission upfront.

Conversely, CFOs tend not to like this because they are taking a risk on each deal. Will the customer stay? To mitigate their discomfort, you could consider a clawback provision on part of the commission if the customer churns before 24 months.

Pay based on customer revenue growth

Expansion revenue is key to growing a subscription business, so you need to decide if you're going to pay salespeople a portion of this revenue bucket. One driver of this decision should be how your buyers typically 'grow.'

For example, if your Customer Success team does a phenomenal job at helping your customers use more and pay more, Sales wasn't needed to make it happen. You might want to consider rewarding the Customer Success team with some kind of a bonus; there is no downside to not compensating Sales in this situation.

On the other hand, if Customer Success identifies customers ripe for upgrading, and then Sales calls the customers and convinces them to do so, Sales is an integral part of the process. In this case, they should probably be compensated.

Impactful Insight

Salespeople are smart. They do what they are incentivized to do. Create your compensation plan wisely.

Ripping off the band-aid — Slowly or Quickly?

Five years from now, you hope to have your business model wholly transitioned to subscription, but do you have to do it all at once? Some companies, like Adobe when they moved its Creative Suite to the cloud, flipped a switch and — almost overnight — their products were no longer available as a perpetual license. They experienced significant pushback from their customers, but they probably transitioned to a subscription model much more quickly because of the fast decision.

On the other hand, you may choose to phase-in the transition. You can offer both the traditional product and the new subscription product simultaneously. New buyers will probably go with the subscription. Existing customers may choose to wait until the new product is more proven. This keeps you from upsetting your most important customers as you have the chance to work out the kinks and build a better product. You can also learn what's important to customers who are using the new solution.

Another key benefit of phasing in the new product is cash flow. You'll recall from chapter 1 that one of the few disadvantages of going with a subscription model is that the initial lack of cash flow is painful. It is even more painful when transitioning a traditional product to a subscription because you're used to a certain level of cash. If you used to get $360,000 per sale, now you're getting approximately $10,000 per month for a subscription fee. It takes about three years to match the cash flow. Phasing in the new subscription product means you'll still be selling the traditional product to some buyers, resulting in some often-needed cash flow.

Pick a goal as to how long you want the transition to take. You may need to tweak the sales compensation plan over the transition period to motivate salespeople to sell according to your plans.

Change management

Given what you've read so far in this chapter on transitioning to a subscription, it is obvious many people inside your company have to change the way they think and behave:

- Salespeople are selling a different product and have a new compensation package.
- Marketing people are not only trying to win customers, but they are also involved in keeping customers and growing customer revenue.
- Product managers must define different products and package them to incentivize upselling.
- Engineering needs to build and provide usage monitoring to help Customer Success and the product team.
- Finance needs to create a whole new set of KPIs to monitor the success of the business.
- Executives need to buy into all of this, plus so much more.

This is not going to be easy. You need to dedicate resources with executive-level backing for the sole purpose of driving the change. Change management is hard — this needs to be a committed project to succeed.

Impact Pricing offers educational programs to help your entire company know what to expect during this transition. We support everyone inside the organization to use the same language and KPI's.

Summary

To be fair, this chapter only touched on some of the many vital decisions and management challenges your company will face as it transitions to subscriptions. Your company will likely require other changes as well. The key is to go into this new journey with your eyes wide open and a flexible attitude. Many functions *must* change. A significant change management process is vital.

EXERCISE 11

Take a moment to list all of the departments and functional areas in your company. Think deeply about each one. Will it have to change? How?
How will you manage it?

12

Billing Systems

———————◆———————

As you transition to a subscription business model, you will almost certainly want to change your billing system. Yes, you've already spent massive resources purchasing and developing your processes and systems, especially around invoicing — but if you stick with those systems, you will have to add many more inefficient and manual processes.

Traditional Billing

For your traditional products, billing isn't overly challenging. The most straightforward case is when you are selling online: you show your price on your website, the buyer pays the price with a credit card, and then you ship the product. It doesn't get any simpler.

It's a little more complicated when companies place orders with other companies. You start by receiving a purchase order for a product, and the purchase order includes the agreed-upon price. You ship the product and immediately send out an invoice with the agreed-upon price on it. Weeks later, the payment comes in, and you reconcile the amount paid with the price on the invoice. This process may not be super simple, but it's a system your accounting department understands and executes well.

Subscription Billing

What changes in the billing process when you launch a subscription product? Well, a lot. This section will go through many processes you can expect to add or change.

Frequency of billing/payment

Instead of billing once and receiving one payment, you must now bill and receive payments periodically. Assuming a monthly subscription plan, you need to send out a request for payment — perhaps by email — and receive the payment every month. Like most subscription companies, you will want to automate this process.

Changing prices

Subscription revenue can change drastically from month to month, even from individual customers. For example, good subscription models motivate customers to upgrade to higher-level packages. This way, those customers will pay more in the next period than before. You've also seen the connection between choosing the right pricing metric and the increase in a customer's usage, which means they pay you more than the previous month. Or, maybe someone wants to downgrade what they purchase, or even cancel altogether. Because of these constant changes, every month, your billing system needs to recalculate what each customer owes before billing them.

Different contract lengths

Some customers will want to pay you month to month. Some will opt for an annual plan. Your billing system needs to keep track of this, too.

Payment methods

You want it to be as easy as possible for your customers to pay you. Instead of having customers send a check or wire transfer after receiving your invoice, it is much easier to pay by credit card or some other method where your customer can pay automatically without thinking about it. After all, they already made the decision — now you're just making it convenient for them.

Changing products

Over time, your product team will change the way you package and offer products. Most companies grandfather in existing customers by not adjusting their plans or prices. Yet all new customers will buy from the new set of product offerings at the latest prices. Therefore, the number of products and prices you bill for each month will increase.

Collection process

This is the process you use to collect unpaid bills. (It's also called the Dunning process.) If your customer is paying with a credit card and the card is declined, what will you do? Was the card reported lost or stolen? Did it expire? Did the subscriber tell the payment processor to stop allowing charges? Issues like this will come up. They may or may not be intentional decisions by your subscriber.

Communication with operations

There needs to be an easy way for operations to tell accounting when a customer has exceeded their limits and needs to pay the price for the next level. Similarly, accounting needs to inform operations when a customer didn't pay, and their access should be shut off. Ideally, this communication should be automated, not an actual conversation.

Impactful Insight

Billing is quite different in subscriptions than for a traditional business. Automate as much as possible.

Vendors

Many software vendors can help with your recurring billing issues. The three I see most often are Chargebee, Chargify, and Zuora (listed in alphabetical order, so you don't think I prefer one). Although I don't recommend one over the other, I highly recommend you buy this capability instead of building it yourself. They have seen and fixed problems your teams haven't even thought of yet. It's a fast-moving market — let the experts do what they do best.

Summary

Billing systems may not be sexy, but they are critical for creating a subscription business. Sending invoices by hand wastes time and money. Reconciling payments does too. Many companies have already solved this problem for you by offering solutions for automating these processes.

EXERCISE 12

Talk to accounting about how you are going to bill your new subscription product. Can they automate most or all of it?

13

Transitioning Customers

———————◆———————

Another unique challenge faced by companies transitioning to subscriptions is handling existing customers who purchased your traditional (non-subscription) product. This is especially true if your customers paid for a perpetual software license, and they currently pay you an annual maintenance fee for updates and upgrades. Your customer bought your product with the expectation they would never have to buy again.

This chapter is about getting those customers to shift to the new subscription product. Let's look at the carrots (incentives) and the sticks (disincentives) you can use to influence customer behavior.

Carrots

I have a strong preference for motivating people to want to switch to our new product. If we give them the right incentives, they may happily adopt the new subscription version of our product. Here are several positive tactics you can use to help convince them.

More problems solved

In chapter 10, you learned you should be building a subscription that offers more benefits than your traditional product. Your subscription offering was created by understanding the ancillary problems surrounding the ones you traditionally solve and finding resolutions to them. This means your entire new subscription platform is a carrot because it does more for your customers than your traditional product by solving more problems for them. You need to be able to explain this clearly to your subscribers.

More benefits in the cloud

Ideally, you solve additional problems with your subscription. Still, if you also take this opportunity to move to the cloud, your new offering has further benefits all your customers can appreciate. For example, you now take on the responsibility for cybersecurity, server acquisition and maintenance, and patches and middleware in the ecosystem. Any IT executive will tell you these are extremely valuable. By moving to the cloud, you are delivering even more benefits to your customers.

Workarounds

If a customer has been using your product for long, they have likely created manual processes to work around any places where your product doesn't perfectly match their way of doing business. These are areas of inefficiency. Often this is caused by the customization they required when you first delivered the product. Hence, as markets and industries change, and your customer's version of your product doesn't keep up, they create workarounds.

During the transition to subscriptions, they now have the chance to clean up many of those workarounds to make their whole system efficient again. It is their chance to have a standard product that will keep up with changes in the market. Many of the customer's workarounds will probably be solved by the additional benefits you added to the subscription product.

Hold your Pricing

With all of these added benefits, who wouldn't want to switch to your new subscription? And yet, salespeople often take the easy route. They say to a customer, "You are already paying us $10,000 per year for maintenance. Let's just make that your subscription price." This is insane! You are now delivering so much more value to your customers by offering a subscription; why shouldn't you get paid for it?

One effective strategy is to not talk about price. Don't talk about their current maintenance fee; talk about the benefits of the transition. Help them understand that the value of what you're offering far exceeds what they currently have. Then, you can talk about the price. People will only pay you more if they believe they are getting more. Help them realize it.

Impactful Insight

Your current customers want the benefits of your new subscription product. You need the courage to charge them for these additional benefits.

Sticks

Hopefully, you can get your current customers to transition based solely on the positive motivations. However, there comes a time when you want to nudge them or maybe even push them, to make the switch. Here are some nudges and pushes, in increasing order of severity.

No new features

To the extent possible, stop developing any new features on the traditional product. They may require some regulatory updates or bug fixes, but as your product teams develop new solutions to new problems, only put those solutions on the subscription product.

This is not drastic to your customers and won't push them to switch quickly, but their incentive to adopt the new product will increase over time.

Raise prices

When you're ready to move even more people to the new platform, raise prices on the current maintenance price (if your contracts allow it). You may even want to give your customers a schedule of future price increases.

They will undoubtedly ask you why. Your answer should be something like, "we have raised our prices because fewer and fewer people are on the old platform, and it costs us much more on a per-customer basis to maintain it." You could also say something like, "the company really wants to discontinue this product, but we decided to keep it available a little longer to support customers like you. However, it would be beneficial to you if you consider switching to our new, superior product."

If you raise prices significantly and quickly, customers will be motivated to switch. If they don't change, at least you are making more revenue.

Discontinuance

The most drastic stick is simply to kill the product. Hopefully, you already stopped selling it to new customers; now, you're going to stop maintaining it. This is the incentive many of your customers need.

After taking all three of these steps, you will likely still have some customers who don't switch. Maybe they don't use your product enough, or they don't see the value. My advice is to stop worrying about these customers. Instead, focus on the new customers and additional revenue you can win due to your new capabilities.

Who moves when?

More good news: you don't have to transition all of your customers at once. You may want to create a list of customers you want to move first, second, and third.

Consider starting with your lowest-risk customers. These are the ones who are using a standard product, meaning no customization. They probably don't pay you a lot. They may even use a defined subsegment of your features. Move these customers first. You don't want to lose them, but it won't be too painful if you do. Then, learn from the experience — what worked? What didn't? Tweak your product and your transition process based on the knowledge you gained.

Next, move the majority of your customers, but not your larger, strategic ones yet. The majority of customers use a standard product and most of your features. Again, learn from the effort and tweak your product and process as needed.

The last customers you want to move are the larger, strategic ones. You probably customized your traditional product for them. They are crucial to your future, and you do not want to lose them. Move them last, as this will give you the best chance to succeed.

Warning: If you move your strategic customers first, there will be many bad outcomes. You will spend the next several years trying to make these few customers happy. You may gain a bad image in the industry. You may even lose many of these customers because the product isn't ready. Don't take such a huge risk — move these customers last.

Summary

This chapter was about transitioning customers from your traditional product to your subscription. It always seems scary when asking a customer to change what they do; in my experience, it isn't nearly as bad as you might imagine. There will likely be less pushback because your customers want the latest capabilities too — they might just need some help getting there.

EXERCISE 13

Create a transition plan to move your current customers onto the subscription platform. What strategies could work for your market? How will you determine the order in which your customers will move to the new product (who moves first, next, and last)?

14

Hardware (and IoT) Challenges

◆

This chapter applies to any hardware company moving to subscriptions, and if this describes your company, you're most likely creating an IoT (Internet of Things) product. This is because most IoT companies adopt a subscription business model. A subscription business may not be a requirement of IoT, but it's a logical fit. After all, an IoT business delivers a continuous stream of benefits *and* likely has a means of measuring usage.

If you're not familiar with IoT, it's a system of computing devices and sensors (with unique identifiers that communicate over a network) without requiring human-to-human or human-to-computer interaction. In 1966, a Ford Mustang did not communicate with anything. However, a 2020 Ford Mustang has many sensors and can send data collected from those sensors to cloud storage. You can also call a service technician who can unlock your car remotely, meaning you can control your vehicle (at least parts of it) remotely. Nest Thermostats and Ring Doorbells are two other popular IoT devices we see in the consumer world.

IoT is not limited to the consumer market; many of the most compelling IoT solutions are commercial applications. Caterpillar uses IoT for its large construction machinery. John Deere uses IoT to help farmers be more efficient. Factories use IoT to aggregate performance information. IoT is all around us.

The software has value!

Most hardware companies I've dealt with don't value their software. The executives likely value it, but somehow the company can't convince everyone that customers should pay for software.

Here's what happens.

Historically, and even today, hardware companies use Cost Plus pricing. Finance loves this because they know they are covering their costs on each sale. While negotiating with buyers, Salespeople realize they can never get the company to agree to a price below their costs. Cost, plus a small margin, becomes a natural floor in the salesperson's mind and the business units.

As these companies build newer products, they realize they can do so much more with software. It could be embedded software, applications running on servers, mobile devices, or even the cloud. They realize this software has value, but they just can't seem to figure out how to capture it. And although some companies will put a price on it, they aren't the majority.

When negotiating a deal, Salespeople learned to see the price floor as the cost plus a small margin. But what's the incremental cost of the software? Almost zero. So, salespeople offer to throw in the software for free so they can win the hardware sale. Someone back in HQ, who has to approve these deals, thinks the same way. "If we want to win this deal, giving away the software is better than deeply discounting the hardware."

This mentality and behavior is a direct result of Cost Plus pricing. If there is one concept I wish I could teach all hardware companies to adopt (OK, all companies), it is value-based pricing. Price based on what your customers are willing to pay, not your costs. You can undoubtedly use cost information to set a price floor you don't want to go below, but all prices should be set by understanding how much value you deliver to your customers.

Your software has value! The software often has more value than the hardware: most hardware products today have embedded software to make the hardware functional. The software, the logic, the smarts have much more value than the physical product. The problem is that the physical product has incremental costs and is often necessary to use the software.

Imagine for a second if software companies used Cost Plus pricing. They couldn't survive. Their marginal costs for everything are close to zero. Yet the phenomenal success of so many software companies demonstrates that buyers are willing to pay for software. Stop giving away your software — and your value — for free!

Impactful Insight

Hardware companies can't seem to charge for software because it has no incremental cost.

Value-based pricing

Once you've adopted value-based pricing, meaning you charge what a customer is willing to pay, you will stop focusing on your costs and instead focus on the value of the solution to your customer. The value comes from both the hardware and the software; the value is the benefit.

Ted Leavitt famously said, "nobody wants a ¼" drill, they want a ¼" hole." Nobody wants your hardware or your software. They want the benefits of having them. You want to think about what those benefits are and how much someone would pay to get them.

Your solution requires both hardware and software, but you should stop selling hardware and software. Sell your results. Sell the benefits. Understand the value you deliver and capture your fair share of that value. Once you start thinking this way, then everything else in this book suddenly becomes more feasible.

In particular, think hard about your pricing metric — what you are going to charge for. Before, you always sold hardware, and maybe some software. But it's probably not what you want to do now. Think about how you deliver value to your customers. What do they value? Why do they want your solution? Then, see if there is a way to tie your pricing directly to what they value.

If you are selling smart water pumps, maybe you want to charge by the amount of water you pump. If you are selling smart farm equipment, perhaps you want to charge by the acreage plowed. (John Deere ties their pricing to the value of the crop produced.) Now is the time to be creative. When you tie your pricing to your customers' value, both parties are happy.

Hardware costs money

Contrary to SaaS companies, hardware and IoT companies have a real Cost of Goods Sold (COGS). These costs must be considered when creating your pricing model and pricing levels.

CFOs are notorious for making sure a company doesn't lose money on any deal. It's a laudable attitude, but it may not be the right one for selling a subscription.

In the traditional business model, CFOs had it easy. Calculate the COGS, make sure the price was higher than the COGS plus overhead, make some money. But this only works when you charge for the hardware. What if you charged for usage instead of the hardware? What if a customer's usage wasn't high enough to pay for the hardware costs? Yes, you can use strategies to eliminate the possibility, but what if you didn't? What if you lost money on a few customers because you can't accurately predict the future, but you made a lot more money on the rest of the customers? This seems like a logical and worthwhile trade-off.

If you think about it, insurance companies are exactly like this. They make money from most of their customers. A few customers make claims — and on most of those claimants, the insurance company loses money — but the total amount lost is small. Overall, the company is quite profitable.

I'm not advocating for losing money on a customer as a general rule. I *am* advocating for you to open your mind to the possibility of tolerating it if it provides you with a far better return overall.

In chapter 11, there is a section titled "Upfront Implementation Costs." Your hardware costs act similarly. To get a new customer started, someone has to take on the cost. As a quick reminder, there were three approaches on how to deal with upfront costs:

1. Charging an implementation fee is an upfront payment to cover your costs; it limits your company's risk but puts the risk on your buyer. 2. Longer contract terms can also cover your costs. 3. The last one we called "trust your process." This is where you may be willing to pay the hardware cost yourself because you trust you will deliver enough value, and most customers will end up paying you far more than your costs overall.

Summary

Hardware companies are notoriously bad at charging for software. Good news: as you shift to subscriptions, you can focus on the pricing metric and not worry about whether you are selling hardware or software. You are selling benefits, and you are selling results. After all, these are what your customers are buying from you.

EXERCISE 14

List the benefits your customers expect to get from your product. Can you find any that you could use as your pricing metric instead of charging for hardware or software?

15

Conclusion

———————◆———————

Congratulations on making it to the end of this book! This demonstrates your commitment to building a great subscription product for your market. Your customers will love you, your investors will love you, and your executives will love you, too.

Studying the subscription business model brought me so many aha moments that I felt I just had to share them in this book. I hope you had many of those same moments while reading it.

My altruistic hope is that you implement what you learned and create a subscription product that grows faster than Zoom, or Slack, or Twilio, or …

After reading through the book, you may have more questions. You may want more detail on how to do something. Impact Pricing offers both live and online education. We also offer programs to help you implement these concepts. You can learn more at www.impactpricing.com.

The subscription business model is amazing. It may not be new, but the adoption of this model by many high-tech companies has allowed many of us to study it and see what works and what doesn't.

Subscriptions are not easy, but they are extremely valuable. Take a chance and try one on your own. You now know more than most people about managing one.

Let's Stay Connected

There is always so much more to learn, especially for me. As I have new aha moments, I typically write about them in my blog. If you want access to my latest learnings and thoughts, here are two ways.

First, send me an invitation on LinkedIn. It is easy to find me. We post all of our free content there and that's where the conversations happen.

Second, go to impactpricing.com and sign up for our newsletter. Then you will receive all of my new free content direct to your email. (LinkedIn doesn't automatically show you all of our content.)

Finally, from time to time we post additional resources about subscriptions. Access these at www.Win-Keep-Grow.com/resources.

About The Author

Mark Stiving is a pricing educator and advisor with a Ph.D. in marketing (pricing) from U.C. Berkeley and more than 25 years of experience helping companies implement value-based pricing strategies to increase profits. A pricing educator and advisor, Stiving has helped esteemed companies like ADP, Cisco, Fiserv, Sabre, Splunk, and ThermoFisher as well as hundreds of small businesses and entrepreneurial ventures. He is the author of the highly rated and readable book Impact Pricing: Your Blueprint For Driving Profits as well as weekly blogs since 2010. Mark hosts the popular podcast called Impact Pricing. See more content from him at www.ImpactPricing.com. Mark lives in Reno, NV with his wife Carol and dog Jake.

A free ebook edition is available with the purchase of this book.

To claim your free ebook edition:

1. Visit MorganJamesBOGO.com
2. Sign your name CLEARLY in the space
3. Complete the form and submit a photo of the entire copyright page
4. You or your friend can download the ebook to your preferred device

Print & Digital Together Forever.

Snap a photo

Free ebook

Read anywhere

9 781631 954788